# INHERITANCE

# &

# LEGACY

*Our Pursuit*

*Of*

*A Narrative,*

*Meaning, Purpose, and Family*

**WRITTEN BY**
**STEPHON DOWNER**

Other books by Stephon Downer


REFLECTIONS OF THE SON


BEHIND THE EYES OF MEN

The Politics of Territory, Space, and Place


INVISIBLE EMPIRE

The Politics of Power, Race, and Resentment


DEATH IN THE DARKNESS

The murder of Carlos Ruiz and the Wrongful Conviction of
Stephon Downer

# INHERITANCE

*is everything our ancestors left to us*

## &

## LEGACY

*is everything we leave to our descendants*

**Stephon Downer**

*******

The Historical factor is the cultural cement that unifies the disparate  elements of a people to make them into a whole, by the particular slant of the feelings of historical continuity lived by the totality of the collective.

The historical conscience, through the feeling of cohesion that it creates, constitutes the safest and  the most solid shield of cultural security for a people. This is why every people  seeks only to know and to live their true history well, to transmit its memory to their descendants.

The essential thing,  for people, is to rediscover the thread that connects them to them to their most remote ancestral past. In the face of cultural aggression of all sort, in the face of all disintegrating factors of the outside world, the most efficient cultural weapon with which a people can arm itself is this feeling of historical continuity.

Cheikh Anta Diop

# Table of Contents

# SECTION I

# THE PURPOSE AND PRESENCE

# OF HISTORY

The preservation of "history" by written documentation, oral tradition or song, are the ways in which people transmit the remembrance of events they found important, or noteworthy. For thousands of years humans carved events on rock walls, and painted scenes in caves; we wrote on parchment, papyrus, stone, bone, clay, paper, and committed to memory everything we believe was important. This preservation of history is done by all societies, on each continent, in every corner of the planet.

History is essentially a people's idea of: what happened; where it happened; whom it happened to; how it happened; and why it happened. It can be based on what we call fact or fiction, or some mixture of them both, and does not necessarily mean truth. Rather, it means *this is what we say happened,* this is our truth and our story. History can cover any subject, but there are a few broad categories always represented. History is always written from the perspective of a family, community, clan, tribe, ethnicity, racial, regional, state, or nation. Both winners and losers have their own version of the facts; however, the winner's version is the story we hear most. History concerns itself with individuals, events, matter, and people. History is the movement, jostling, and shifting of humanity; it is the clash of ideas and armies over space. History is the birth, rearing, joy, suffering, and deaths of generation after generation of men, woman, and children, that keeps the world moving forward, within this reality we call time.

The concept of history is the intellectual act of linking groups of people to a body of phenomena, through time and space - and ascribing meaning to it. Every people on earth have the concept of history embedded into the fabric of their culture, which shows how important to our species. We are driven to connect everything that came before us to the present moment. History serves many purposes, the most important of which is to fulfill our need to feel connected to something greater. We learn history in order to maintain an infinite conversation with the people who came before us; in order to know why their ghosts continue to roam the planet long after they are gone. We learn to heed their warnings, laugh at their humor, contemplate their tragedy, and learn from their lessons. No matter how hard we may try, there is no such thing as 'only the now.' Humans simply cannot live in an ahistorical limbo, and still remain grounded in reality. There must be a physical and metaphysical beginning and end; and it is from this we derive all other meanings in life. Those who deny the relevance of history, to our modern sense of self, do so to their own peril. For some ancient and unknown reason, in order to find meaning in their life, our human ancestors always looked behind them for the answers.

There is no escape from the clutches of the past, even for the modern technologically-sophisticated man. Everyone is bound by tradition, including the most powerful down to the weakest; whether he be CEO of a multi-billion-dollar company, or a bushman whose people have lived the same way for thirty thousand years. All people are in some way shackled to the constitutions, laws, traditions, and customs written and practiced centuries ago. Those who wish to stake their claim to any right must point to an old clause and phrase ratified, signed, or spoken into law by a legislative body who has been dead for too long for anybody to remember. All kings and every prophet had to tie their legitimacy to an age that passed before them.

Even our modern laws rests on the deeds, actions, and decisions of people who lived in an ancient past.  In 2004 the United States Supreme Court in <u>Crawford v. Washington</u> reaffirmed that a defendant had a Sixth Amendment right to "Confront his accusers" in court. Interestingly, the Supreme Court traces the modern *"...right to confront one's accuser... [to] a concept that dates back to Roman times."*1 This is nothing new, both Jews and Muslims are completely governed by ancient books, and heavily rely on medieval sources to settle modern problems. The Jew has his Torah, Mishnah, and Gemera; and the Muslim  the Qur'an, Hadeeth, Sharia, and Islamic Fiqh (jurisprudence/ law). Those who claim not to care about history, nonetheless, find themselves bound by it and citing it when it benefits their cause or case.

## CONCEPT OF HISTORY/HISTORICAL NARRATIVE

The concept of history comprises four parts: 1) the world before man; 2) the creation of man; 3) the world after man was created; and 4) man's present state of affairs. What humans call 'history' includes: man's beliefs about the creation of the world prior to his origins; and all that has happened since<u>. Including everything that happened leading up to his present condition; and how these events relate to his present reality.</u> *<u>What people think about their collective past is inseparable from their thinking about their present. Their ideas about their history shapes their politics.</u>2*

# IN THE BEGINNING

PREHISTORY THE BEGINNING OF HUMANS

&

THEIR CREATION AND PLACEMENT ON EARTH

The 'western' Black male's concept of "the beginning" has two paths to the past. The first is rooted in the religious doctrines of Judaism, Christianity, and Islam. Which proposes the belief that before God created man and animals, only God and his angels existed. Islam believes that Jinns also existed prior to man, and the state of this existence, and its time period, is beyond the comprehension of men. According to the Judaic, Christian, and Islamic traditions God created man from mud or clay, and life was breathed into him by an entity (god or angel). In these stories woman was created at separate time, from man's rib. This dates back, thousands of years, to an Egyptian creation story; except in the Egyptian version man and woman were created together from clay.

It is difficult to know what people really think on any subject. However, as it pertains to belief in the ancient past, a considerable portion of Black males, who are religious, believe that the Garden of Eden is where life for man on earth has its origins. First man is created (somewhere other than earth) and then placed in the Garden of Eden, where he lived a life free of struggle and hardship.

Then, because of their (Adam and Eve's)  disobedience they were forced out of Eden. This is where the historical narrative becomes fuzzy. Those who believe this tradition rely only on a small body of religious literature from which to draw all their conclusions. For them, only the stories found in religious text have historical relevance. These stories contain all the wisdom that they think is essential, everything outside religious literature is considered unimportant.

The second "creation story" that is widely held is rooted in conspiracy theories - old and new alike - that have recently gained mainstream traction. This includes some version of the belief that extra-terrestrials played some role in the human presence on earth. Some believe that we as humans began  as an extraterrestrial experiment of some kind.  There is a whole body of quasi-scientific/ quasi-historical literature on the subject. A picture begins to emerge where those who reject religious creation stories,  nonetheless, feel the need to believe something, and go on to fill this need to believe with  popular, but unsubstantiated, theories. Ideas that have been floating around for decades find a home in the fertile imaginations of the disillusioned, educated,  and un-educated.

Many are in search of a narrative  they believe has been hidden from them. They  believe the truth is now being revealed to those enlightened  enough to understand. There is an industry of conspiracy-theory television and media that peddle ideas of 'ancient aliens,' UFOs, and visitors from another planet. Which are popular and have a cult-like followings. Ironically, those who claim to reject the religious explanations of human origins, nonetheless, reference religious text whenever possible support their own beliefs; by blending selective passages of  religious text (historic myths) found in "holy books" with modern fringe theories. Obscure and incomplete statements or in myths or scenes found on temple walls are turned into proof of some grand theory about our collective past. Again, religion may have lost its cachet to many, but if one looks and listens they will find religious myths, precepts, and dogma mixed with modern (political) conspiracy theories. These helter-skelter concepts, scatter-brained as they are, make-up the world of modern belief systems of the masses and form a tower of Babel in their minds. Figuring into the worldview of modern believers are:

Aliens,

Freemasons,

the Illuminati,

Rockefellers,

Rothschilds,

J.P. Morgan,

the Bilderberger group,

the Trilateral Commission,

the international Zionist Jews,

and an assortment of Eastern religions and philosophies including Indian (Buddist & Hindu) and     Asian (Chinese & Japanese) beliefs

Christianity,  Judaism, Islam, in all their strains and various beliefs

All Western Governments and their allies  are diabolical

Globalism /globalist

Conservative agenda

Liberal agenda

Oil companies

Pharmaceutical industry


       People take their conspiratorial ideas about these groups, and combine them with their own national politics, and historical (racial or ethnic) grievances. Confused white men concoct conspiracies to fit some preconceived agenda, while Blacks form their own warped opinions about what is true. Each group and individual has the capacity to form a complex belief system. Everything floating in the cultural ether is blended together to form a unified theory about life, living, and the world order. Every single idea they've come into contact with constitutes part of a convoluted personal philosophy - that makes sense only to the beholder. There are now so many versions of 'the truth' it would take a computer to unravel them.

This shows humans cannot exist without forming a narrative about themselves and their place in the world; and will manufacture psychological order from the chaos that exist around them. The only consistent theme found in all conspiracy theories is that everyone, no matter their belief, believes that the other is out to get them.

As it pertains to the secret societies, capitalist, and political groups named above, they are seen as the cause of every natural disaster and all political turmoil - spanning centuries. They are believed to be the movers behind scenes, in every evil intrigue; and the invisible hand behind random global phenomenon like: wars, market crashes, coups, and viral disease pandemics. While religions and spiritual philosophies are used to explain unseen phenomenon, suffering, and aspects of the human condition - that cannot be articulated. In order to keep its message relevant to a modern audience, religion is used to explain present-day political phenomenon; while religious text are being used to interpret geo-political moves, made by contemporary leaders.

When Russia, China, America, or Arabians makes a move there are people who cannot interpret their actions, except through the lens of scripture. This is a very primitive and symbolic way to gaze at the world; and distorts the truth of our material existence, and its complexity. Nobody can understand modern-day Middle East politics by only studying ancient or medieval Islamic literature; there is no way to comprehend the Palestinian or Israeli conflicts by reading the *Old Testament*; there is no way to grasp modern Egyptian politics by reading *The Book of the Dead* papyrus, or a preserved report written by a pharaoh; there is no way to appreciate India's political situation by reading the Vedas; and there is no way to understand the modern politics of Greece or the Mediterranean by reading the *Iliad*.

When America is seen only as "Babylon" and Russia "Magog" the person is no closer to understanding  the actual (politkal, or economic) inner workings of these governments. These are simply religious terms that denote the empire is powerful, evil, and ungodly; this description  contains absolutely no knowledge of the structure of  these governments. That is to say, the terms are useless as information, and can only be used to invoke fear and hatred. It is absurd to take the two thousand year old propaganda found on temple walls, and other religious narratives, and develop a clear concept of today's world.

The modern world is impossible for anybody to digest as a whole. It must be absorbed piecemeal and  conceptualized in its parts, before we can begin to achieve even a vague outline of its composition. The ancient past is even more difficult to comprehend, because of the long passage of time and incomplete historical record. Those who fail to realize this want to oversimplify our complex existence - because the truth is hard  to find, harder to face, and people find it impossible to say: "I don't know," when they have no clue.

Ancient men lived in a very small world. They were concerned with their idols, gods, serpents, and spirits. Their ancestors, pharaohs, the darkness, disease, and Romans were blamed for every bad thing in the world. Whereas today's cluttered mind is occupied with similar problems, in addition to, their modern counterparts to blame. Today's masses have more knowledge of the world than those who came before them; as a consequence, they have to process and try to make sense of much more data about the nature of reality. They must make sense of both the ancient past and the modern present, only guided by fragments of religious lore, conjecture, fact, fiction, and the unknown. Today's mind must grapple with both religion and science, truth and instinct, information overload and lack of understanding. As such, most people possess a kaleidoscope of beliefs, most of which are contradictory or rooted in speculation. Therefore, very few are able to develop a narrative about humanity or theory of life, grounded in a factual historical record, pure science, or verifiable data.

Until recently, the theory of evolution being accepted as an historical truth, biological fact, and scientific reality is a complete nonstarter for 99.5% of Black males. The idea that we descended from a primitive species is rejected; and anyone who adopts the theory openly get strange looks. The questions of human origins is a touchy topic that makes everyone uncomfortable. The subtext to any discussion of evolution is that: 'it is some shit white people wants us to believe.' The evidence of prehistoric man's existence, in the form of primitive (or fossilized) bones found around the world, makes for an uncomfortable conversation. There are many who simply refuse to entertain the question and say 'I don't know and I don't care,' when asked about the origins of humans.

That is to say, very few arrive at their conclusions based on research and investigation of scientific theories. Generally speaking, to discuss the theory of evolution - in any of its stages - makes Black males uncomfortable. Those committed to a religious understanding of the world understand that evolution conflicts with the tenets of all major religious doctrines, and will never let such an idea disrupt the mental concepts that bring them peace of mind.

Notwithstanding, the person offended by the idea of evolution need not be religious. I know plenty who do not believe in the god of the Bible, yet still find the concept of 'evolution' an absurd premise to begin with. When pressed to explain where we came from some say: "we've always been here." If pressed further to elaborate on the diversity of life and species, they become elusive and annoyed. Dinosaurs represent a major conundrum. Furthermore, DNA science is not taken into consideration when it is used to prove the genetic descent of humans.

# EGYPTIANISM

In the fifteenth and sixteenth  centuries, Europe  not only began to colonize  most of the world, but also instituted a systematic colonization of information about the world.

John Henrik Clarke

The African historian who evades the problem of Egypt is neither modest nor objective, nor unruffled; he is ignorant, cowardly, and neurotic.

Cheikh Anta Diop

Egypt  and the rest of Africa  plays a part in Black people's world-view of themselves and their past. Ancient Kemet,  Ethiopia, Kush, Mali, and Ghana to many represents the apex of classical Black-African civilization. Although I have met very few who would cite or rely on Egyptian or African creation myths to explain our human origins,  nonetheless,  there  are  Afrocentric  or  Egyptiancentric concepts that play a strong role in Black cultural thought.

Black historians should be proud that their struggle - which began as far back as the 1880s  - to resurrect the Egyptian past and place it firmly within the family of African civilizations has had great success.  The idea of Black Egypt as the  fountainhead of all civilizations (including western civilization) has penetrated the minds of Blacks of every class in America. It is a history that they guard with great intellectual dexterity, and have much literature on the subject.

The Egyptian fetish is harmless  to say the least. The only true down-side I gather is  that some completely obsess over the subject of Egyptian antiquity and come to know little else regarding their past, or any past for that matter. There is a narrow-mindedness which develops in the minds of men who study the ancient past. They become myopic in vision and thought and treat the study of the past as a new religion; drawing too many (or too few) conclusions about the relevance of the ancient past to the present.

In any case, Black scholarly interest in Egypt and Ethiopian civilization began in the late 19th century; when new scientific disciplines like Anthropology, Archeology, and Egyptology were emerging. And literature on these topics was being produced by the volume. Black scholars soon had to contend with European historians, and their deliberate distortions of African history (world history); using racist scholarship Europeans attempted to systematically write Blacks out of the genesis of  history, and deny that Blacks participated in building human civilization. This was done in order to support their (legal and moral) justification for imperialist expansion, slavery, and genocide (now called "colonization"). Which was a calculated move to make themselves (Europeans & Americans) the new center of the universe. For the sake of clarity, we must begin in Greece and Rome.

The European elite's infatuation with Greek and Roman civilization began in earnest in the 15th century Renaissance,  and quickly gave birth to the concept of the Humanities. Which is the study of human culture, literature, history, art, and philosophy. Within the 'Humanities' Greeks and Romans - in particular- are exalted as the architects of western civilization. Europeans drew a historic linear line from ancient Greece and  Rome directly to themselves; suggesting that they (thousands of years  after the fact) were the direct inheritors of the legacy of these long vanished civilizations.

Whether this is true or false, Europeans imposed upon the rest of the world the idea that ancient 'classical' art, literature, architecture, culture, myths, and history was a standard to be envied. Out of the study of the ancient past Egypt came into the sights of Europeans,  resulting in Napoleon's expedition into the African continent in the late 18th Century (1798). He went with the aim of pillaging, uncovering, and cataloging Egyptian material culture and secrets which were then buried under the sands.  Europeans then added Egypt (the modern territorial state and its ancient heritage) to the list of things they usurped and claimed as their own.

To accomplish this white-washing they had to deny what was in front of their eyes. The Black and brown faces depicted on the walls of the temples had to be ignored, and the written records of ancient scholars (including Greeks) testifying to the Blackness of Egyptians had to be explained away. The truth conflicted with the Eurocentric worldview; which holds, to this day, that Blacks had never created "high culture" or civilization. From this point of view Black people enter world history only as slaves, and were destined to be conquered and subject to the will of white men - which was legally justified and morally necessary. This false narrative had/has many believers who benefit from this belief.

To counter this propaganda Black & white scholars sprang into action, by pointing out (as early as the 1870s) that the Egyptians were Africans and the proof was plainly visible and supported by the historical record of their contemporaries. These scholars highlighted that, contrary to propaganda,  Africans had not only created "high culture" but initiated the longest lasting and  sophisticated civilization of the ancient world. And this was done thousands of years before much of the world - including Northern Europeans - had given up barbarism and nomadic living. These scholars argued that: Black Egyptians had given civilization to others, including the Greeks, and that this was attested to by the Greeks themselves.

Therefore if the same logic of the Europeans is used, the linear  line of history that extended from the Greeks and Romans should (must) extend further back to the Egyptians. Ipso facto it is the Blacks who  created the first model (modern) civilization, and the world has inherited this concept from them.  A second, but equally important, point is that Black scholars reject the idea that Greco-Roman literature, architecture, music, art, and mythology are the cultural apex of the ancient world. A credible body of  historical scholarship has been produced because of these debates, and dishonest historians have been checkmated academically.

That being said, people absorbed with Egyptian  literature often immersed themselves in topics of (lost) ancient knowledge, philosophy, and mystical (or alien) technologies. Very often subpar literature, of questionable scholarship, is bought by those seeking enlightenment. In an effort to acquire the wisdom of the ancients, esoteric books about symbols and mysticism are highly valued. It is believed that such knowledge has the power to unlock unknown dimensions or higher planes of understanding. People who obsess over this sort of literature believe there is a shortcut to acquiring scientific proficiency or philosophical enlightenment.

They think the path to illumination will come to them by reading books full of riddles and mysterious words, or through the ability to decipher very subjective scriptures - which can be interpreted a thousand different ways. They believe they will become higher beings and achieve intellectual clarity by penetrating the world of mystery. Ultimately they want to become agents of change, but from a metaphysical standpoint opposed to a mechanistic. My conclusion is that they want to become powerful holy men or false prophets;  they do not want to be engineers, scientist,  or generals, they want to be gurus.

They want to possess 'the secrets of the ancients' and unlock new dimensions of the universe, and imagine these secrets are obtained overnight by stumbling on to the right book or scripture. Although they are highly motivated to learn,  they remain misguided because the study of esoteric subjects will never bring a cluttered mind into sharp focus. Furthermore, the study of dead men and old buildings will gain us nothing if we cannot bring order to our present situation  and solve modern problems.

In any case, lower class Blacks have many more distractions, as a consequence, their cultural attention has shifted from the esoteric subjects to an obsession with materialism; as such interest in historic literature or ancient knowledge is now atypical.

# HISTORY – A TOOL OR A WEAPON?

Many men long for an idealized past (fact or fictional) whether it be Egyptian, Teutonic, Viking, Native American, Taino Indian, or the 7th century Islamic Mujahedeen. Nostalgia is a powerful tool and device for inspiring men because humans do not exist in a limbo. People understand that they themselves are simply links in a chain and part of a larger narrative - nature, culture, and logic teaches this. The basis of many pre-Christian religions, on every continent, throughout the world was (in many cases still is) based on ancestor worship. It is even thought that gods began as ancestors who had long died, but were believed to still protect over the tribe and who were eventually deified by later generations.

Whatever the case, the glories of the past are powerful symbols and points of focus for all groups of people; especially those living in uncertain times. Instinctively people feel the need to point back and say "it was better back in the day." For this reason groups who are presently upset over some local, national, or geopolitical issue all say the same thing: it was better back then. The dumbest of them then strive to get back to this "better" time, while the worst of them try and make the present a replica of the past. Listen to any political speech, they always promise their resentful audience: we will make it great again. Republicans want it to be the 1950s (or 1861) and Democrats the 1990s.

Many use history to wipe away feelings of inferiority, by pointing to dead men who they believe embodied ideal values and the best example of manliness. After which they then claim or invent some (genetic, spiritual, or philosophical) connection to these men as if they themselves are a continuation of this person's legacy, or the person who must fulfill the divine mission of the dead man. The subtext being, there is a pure state of man that we have gotten away from; whose essence and substance we must achieve once more. And the only way to bring this pure state of man back is to return to the "good old days" and do things like they were done in the past - by emulating those who laid the foundation.

It is a common belief that humans, as a species, have strayed from their original righteous path; and that we were once great and then descended into something worse. Those who subscribe to such ideas, naturally, want to learn the secrets of the past and use them to resurrect this fallen man of today. I find a common thread in all of their logic is that the modern world is too complicated, and they would rather retreat into the past which they view as a simpler (more pure) time. White males want to retreat into a simpler time where barbarian logic reigned supreme, and blacks want to retreat to a time when righteous men (Kings) ruled over the masses. Both are misguided in their simplistic view of the past, their ideas of human nature, and the development of modern society. The truth of the matter is that man probably began as something much worse and slowly ascended into something more interesting.

The Black men I encounter, who obsess over history and the past, are not particularly focused on self mastery; they do not want to learn artistry, mathematics, engineering or technological expertise. Rather, they want a power that is more elusive, maybe even shamanistic. Black males (and others) use the study of the past as a security blanket, to feel safe and warm inside, and give them some pride about themselves. Yet many of them are not inspired enough to build anything - neither institution, movement, nor structure. They revel in the thoughts of Black empires and pyramids, but dare not attempt to actualize them. This is impotence in the larger scheme of things; the level of their obsession with the past is an indicator of how empty they feel inside.

Through  books and other media they imagine and dream of another past, a different world, a better place, and alternate history. In this sense, history (like religion) resembles opium. But ultimately man must come down from this euphoria and face his present situation and all its disappointments, by finding modern solutions to his age old dilemmas. Studying history is a useful tool for finding patterns, borrowing strategies, predicting behavior, and analyzing missteps, but has many limitations. We must always approach the world with a fresh set of eyes, and make decisions based on contemporary circumstances and realities.

# NATIONALISM

The study of history, in some cases, has a narrow nationalist agenda. Nationalism itself is a legitimate political philosophy that harnesses the frustration of a population, by channeling anger and raw energy, in order to unleash its creativity. Nationalism focuses on the economic, cultural, and political self-interest of a racial or ethnic group. Economic independence (economic power), cultural chauvinism (cultural supremacy), and political aggression (selfishness) is at the heart of all nationalist movements. The high-minded morality that members of the group or tribe apply to each other need not be applied to others; who are viewed as potentially hostile outsiders - and at the very least competitors. The leader says to them: *'only we matter, everyone else is of little importance; whatever happens to them is of no concern to us; those other people may or may not be our enemies, it all depends on what they can do for us. Only we who look like this, come from here, and believe this way are important.'*

The nationalistic sentiment of a population is cultivated through the use of history (mythology/ legends), grievance propaganda, and symbolism. Leaders within the group first manufacture one group from many (e Pluribus Unum), and then develops a collective sense of shared history and destiny. The nationalist leader communicates with all classes and religions; and convinces them that their fates are linked together in a spiritual and historical bond, that cannot be broken except by betrayal or death.

That said, there is a major difference between white nationalism and other nationalisms.

White nationalism has always been a predatory philosophy; whose aim is the subjugation of brown people. Whereas Black nationalism and other nationalist groups - whether Asian, Latin, or African - were born out of the need to resist white subjugation. There has never been a struggle for independence, against racial or colonial oppression, that has not been led through a nationalist uprising. Even battles that appear to be over religion are often nationalist insurgencies couched in religion; the Taliban vs. the United States and the West is a case in point.

Nationalism is unstable and volatile by its very nature, it has gotten a bad name because it has been misused by megalomaniacs to commit violence en masse (Nazism was a nationalist movement). Extreme nationalist study the past with the specific aim of exalting themselves (the nation/ folk/volk) above others, while discrediting or devaluing everyone else. He is not looking for truth he is searching for validation, and affirmation of his greatness. Anything that negates this belief is written out of history and erased from his mind. He is always in pursuit of a prehistoric man untainted by contact with others. For the fanatical nationalist everyone else is inferior and dirty - physically, spiritually, and morally- and contact with them does more harm than good. The glorification of self always accompanies nationalism. Discrediting and devaluation of others requires a group to constantly look backwards; concentrating on old injuries or conflicts, and focusing on their collective self-interest exclusively. They feed their hate intellectually, and are consumed by the thought of what others did or didn't do to them.

In the end, most build nothing with their hate, not even themselves, and certainly not their 'people.' They are people who simply keep one foot in the past and one in the present, and use history as their weapon. The nationalist wants to destroy the world and create future paradise from the bones and ashes of what is left, because the present does not reflect their vision of what the world should be.

Nationalism is one part history, one part politics, one part love of the people, and one part hate of everyone else; it is a political tool or potential weapon that must be used wisely or else its logical conclusions can spell doom for others or yourself. Of all of my political beliefs, nationalism is the one I question most. Moderation and nationalism are difficult to balance; once you begin teaching people about their history in to order uplift and inspire them with pride, they take such information and turn it into hate and resentment of others. I am reluctant to engage the immature mind with ideas that will inflame them and consume them with hatred. On the other hand who am I to determine to what level of extremism is necessary in order to wake a dead mind from its slumber? Learning, teaching, and preaching is a delicate task; it should only be done by level headed teachers, who understand the potential pitfalls of spreading an ideology that may take on a life of its own.

I find that few are able to learn about themselves without coming away with an exalted sense of self and devaluation of others. Teaching a people their history in a positive light has clear psychological and emotional benefits, but it also has negative set backs; people become stupid, narrow-minded, and seem unable to make the distinction between pride in self and contempt of others. But what are the alternatives? In a world where we have been taught to believe we were nothing, and all of our contributions to humanity erased from academic record and memory, history must be used to raise the consciousness of those with depression and amnesia. We have forgotten our roots and been scattered across diasporas, in many ways we have lost the ability to organize on the basic level, and need an ideology that will help us see ourselves as one nation and bind us together in a historical sense. There is no ism like nationalism, it has the ability to bring people of all ethnicities together under one flag; only through nationalism can a diverse population transcend their differences in gender, culture, religion, class, caste, or even race.

That said, as teachers we must acknowledge that nationalism is very dangerous because nobody can control how the student will accept their new teachings or understand the correct amount of animosity that is required to motivate a nation without inadvertently sparking genocidal thoughts. In nationalism there must exist 'the other' who is not you, the question for those who teach cultural or economic nationalism is: how does the 'other' fit into our story without being demonized? And is this possible?

# AHISTORIC MAN/
# OR
# THE MAN WITHOUT HISTORY

"The unhistorical and the historical are equally needed for the health of the individual, a people and a culture." In everyday language: men must "know how to forget at the right time as well as how to remember at the right time".3

Make way for the nihilist who sees nothing but what is before his eyes. Behold, the male with no history! I frequently encounter a Black male who has no concept of time, space, past, or future. He lives for the now in the most absolute sense; his desires, his city, project, his clothes, or block is the beginning and end of his universe. For him there is no linear or cyclical time, only the "now" time - the "I am hungry" time. There is no concept of personal, familial, or collective legacy because that requires a view of the future. Life and death (his or yours) is nothing.

Nothing is sacred. Nothing has value except the material items that makes him feel good; feeling good is his objective. He has no regard for consequence because thought of consequence requires a glimpse into the future. He is mysterious; he has no racial consciousness and exists in human limbo. This male is impenetrable. He conforms to no cultural paradigm; and may be a new species, or a modern version of an old species - prehistoric man as he existed before literature and philosophy. Love is something he cannot admit to; he feels, but not much.  He is hollow, unstable, and dangerous. He has no past and no future. His favorite words are: '*I don't care.*'

# BLACK HISTORY

Black history is more than American history; it is more than  the history of one Island,  country, or  continent; it is world history and history of the world. It  is not a sad history or  tragic history, but a history of peaks and valleys. It is the history of civilization itself; and the history of many civilizations. Black history is the history of primordial man; it is a history of life and death, of struggle  and perseverance. A history  of fighting, warriors  and war.

It is a history of man, woman, and child and a history of many births; i.e., the birth of humanity, of law, of justice, mathematics, science, technology, philosophy, religion, and the spirit world. It is a history of bondage, resistance, and  inspiration. It is a history of destruction and recreation; and of hurdles, obstacles, barriers, and overcoming. It is a  history of transcending and redefining. Black history is a history of building and rebuilding, of movement and migration; a history of blood, song and dance.

This is a history of laughter, music, poverty, and richness. A history of  poetry and legends. It is history of wandering, settlement, soil, and toil. A history of building and destroying; of losing, searching and finding. A history of loss and restlessness; a transformational history of invention, creativity, adaptation and mastery. A history of  gods; a history of Osiris, Isis,  Horus, Christianity, Islam, Ogun, Legba, and Orishas.   The history of hundreds of deities whose attributes live on but whose names are lost to antiquity. Black history is a history of now, today, and tomorrow. Black history is the future, and  an eye-witness to eternity.

It cannot be denied that the study of history is an important aspect of learning for any group, especially for a people who have been culturally obliterated like Blacks in America and worldwide. Our study of history is unlike most other groups; for us, studying history  means we are setting out to reclaim a past that has been deliberately hidden and suppressed. In America the study of the past is a politically subversive act, delving into our past means that we are in pursuit of secrets, crimes, and criminals. When African Americans study history it inevitably leads to uncovering State secrets, and to the dark chapters in the lives of powerful families, communities, and institutions.

All of American history leads back to a crime scene and shattering myths of elite families and  cherished institutions is dangerous business. We are in the process of  salvaging a past that has been buried by an empire that denied our humanity. What has been lost we can never get back. We can only bear witness and do our best to preserve the names and dates of their deeds; so that our book of life may record  the men and women who deserve honorable mention  and those who get the mark of  shame.

We are a complex people and have a story to tell of achievements and setbacks. Our genius has  been forgotten and unacknowledged for too long. Evidence of our creativity and contributions has been suppressed, usurped, denied, and ignored. We must reclaim our stories as proof of our resilience; as such,  it is our duty alone  to make sure our story is preserved for posterity. In order for them to understand the continuity of our struggle,  from then to now, and give context to the situation we find ourselves in.  Each generation of our children must  know our roots and sacrifice,  and understand that only through blood do all things happen.

They must understand we are not a silly people, or a small people, or a foolish people - but  a dynamic and brave community. Our history is sacred and cannot be left to others to explain or document; furthermore we cannot allow it to be  swallowed up in the narratives of others.  Each generation must make its own history, while still preserving and recalling what has come before it. When we tell our story  we do not have to sit around discussing our oppression from dusk till dawn, seething with resentments at past, and present injuries. Too many people detour from the study of Black history and instead fall into an obsessive research of their tormentors. They deviate from the pursuit of knowledge of (the collective) self and instead engage in  a pathological pursuit of white crimes against Black bodies. In doing so they forsake their ancestor's sacrifice, by becoming victims. They never achieve knowledge of themselves because they begin to equate Blackness with victimhood and never know much about Black people, except the bad things that happened to us. In truth, white people become their neurotic  objective.

Hating white people is not a necessary condition of resisting our condition. Generally speaking, it is fine to have a low opinion of people who use their power to oppress others. However, such people come in all colors. Hating all the people of any group just because they are part of that group is absurd on its face, and reflects a narrow minded point of view that fails to recognize the complexities of people and life. Furthermore, hating is tiresome and energy consuming, not to mention stressful and self-destructive. On the other hand, hating is easier and more natural than thinking deeply about the humanity of others.

Suppressing hate and resentment is an extraordinary feat for some who contemplate the depths of our pain. As for those who succumb to the  fire of hate I have no legitimate argument to silence them; I will not tell others what they are supposed to feel. But for myself I cannot sit around hating people all day; I  have to  live, laugh,  plan, work, think, and contemplate. There is physics, law, engineering and biology to study; there are Russian and Japanese novels to read, and finance to master; there are cities, governments, and businesses to run. Some of us have to critique the empire and prepare the next generation to fight; some have to monitor geopolitics (global game of thrones) and strategize; some of us have to remain sober-minded while the rest move about in their feelings.

Understanding the good, sad, and beautiful of Black history with clarity is the aim. We have real political battles to wage against this American machine. We are fighting on multiple fronts. Not only are we  fighting internal battles with ourselves and external battles with our enemies, we are waging a war for the spirit and the flesh of our people, against the rulers of darkness. History teaches us that we can never depend on American institutions to deliver us justice, equality, or freedom without a fight; and freedom goes hand and hand with our blood sacrifice. History has shown us we can never move forward without giving something up.

The study of history must be for drawing inspiration, strength, and to achieve deeper insight; so that we can arrive at unity of purpose. And to preserve and transmit positive techniques for coping with life. We study to know the ways of the righteous, that are tried and true, and the ways of the wicked, that are false. We study history to understand the issues that others had to confront, and how they were resolved. By examining the origin, nature, and parts of our human institutions we can discover the problems that affect every generation. This way we know the common denominator underlining all human phenomena from past to present. We study to know the movements and methods of men, to discover the motives behind their madness.

It is only through the lens of history can we see that blood, knowledge, wealth, and power are the four corners of the human contract; they are inseparable from the human condition. Contrary to what people may say, history is easiest thing to teach. Living your truth is the only way to keep your people's past alive. By being a living example you demonstrate what a thousand books cannot articulate. Our breath, speech, and  action is life - books, paper, and ink are only tools. The screens we watch and the data we consume are dead unless they teach us lessons. We must be on guard, if we do not use history to help us live it will become a yoke that chains us to the past. We must watch the world like Janus, never taking our eyes off the future, but remembering everything in the past.

# OUR ORIGINS, OUR PAST, OUR PRESENT AND FUTURE

"A people with absolutely no memory of their past would be unable to govern themselves successfully, to abide by a proven way of life, and to keep the law; a culture with no traditions, with no memory of past techniques or customs, would be similarly incapacitated. On the other hand, a people or culture without the ability to forget would be unable to make decisions, to act, and to be creative."[4]

The "New World" Americas (the land masses and islands of the Caribbean) was the meeting places where Africans of different clans, ethnicities, customs and religions were forced under the pressures of bondage "soil, work, and danger" to become one people. Each country and island in the Americas produced a distinct Black culture out of the fragmented shards of African ethnicities and families.

These distinct cultures have their own forms of music, dance, language, religion, and logic - and in many cases their own distinct look. The people calling themselves "African American" or "Black" began as a political, genetic and cultural entity on the plantations of the Americas within the last 400 years. Unless a person or family are recent migrants from the continent of Africa, they can trace their lineage, and cultural heritage to the slave systems that existed on the continental United States, Caribbean islands or (to a lesser extent) South America.

The vast majority of Blacks in America trace their roots to the southern states, where the mass of our ancestors met and formed a new culture, while still in bondage. Families and their footsteps can be traced back through our many different migrations. First, by people who escaped plantation life, under the cover of darkness, and made it to Northern and Midwest cities. Secondly, by People who fled the south in waves, fleeing the social prisons erected around them after emancipation. They, too, moved in the darkness guided by only the moonlight and hope, spreading across the U.S. in search of freedom. Driven by desperation and ambition we stampeded new cities and towns in every state.

We now find ourselves, a hundred sixty five years after emancipation, occupying every corner of the United States and every station in  life. We have traveled so far that our ancestor would not have believed it was possible, but we are still on the move and ascendant. Our experience within these American institutions have had a profound effect in shaping our character, psychology, and world view. American logic is very crude, and  has left us with a myopic concept of what it means to be Black, and who fits into that category. It is easy to forget (when it is deliberately not taught) that Jamaicans, Haitians, Dominicans,  Puerto Ricans, Trinidadians, Brazilians, Barbadians, and  Blacks born in the U.S. have common cultural and genetic origins.

Each nation was forged in a unique social, environmental, political, economic, religious, and genetic climate. The only thing that separates us is hundreds of years of evolution; this process took centuries of relative isolation from one another. However, we are not so far apart and contact has never been broken; so when distant cousins meet again and assimilate it is done with little friction. African Americans, when telling our story, often ignore the influx of foreign born Blacks that have immigrated to this country, within the last hundred years,  and been absorbed into the greater political body.

It is often overlooked by native African-Americans just how much Blacks & Latinos, from other parts of the Americas, have contributed to Black culture - dating back over a hundred years. We only need to look at New York City, which is not only the 'culture capital' of the world but, (for decades) the Black culture capital. In terms of its influence on Black (read global) music, dance, art, style, language, literature, poetry, and aesthetic it has no equal. However, it is rarely pointed out that this creativity was formed in an ethnic melting pot. Atlanta Georgia is the new "Black mecca" and other economic and cultural hubs have increased this synthesis of cultures and ethnic assimilation.

Those who laid the foundation for this synergy of creativity were Blacks from the American south and West Indian immigrants from the Caribbean islands/ former British and French colonies. The number of famous New York rappers with foreign born parents and grandparents should make us consider the accuracy of our collective history: Kool Herk, Notorious B.I.G., 50 Cent, Busta Rhymes, Nicky Minaj and many more. Jamaican patois was a common feature of rap music during Hip Hop's "golden era" 1988 - 1998; reminding us of just how much is owed to this influx of new blood and creativity.

The Universal Negro Improvement Association (U.N.I.A.) started in 1919, by Jamaican immigrant Marcus Garvey has no equal. U.N.I.A's members were made up of both West Indians, but its membership were mostly American born Blacks. In terms of a self-affirming philosophy and symbolism it has an enduring influence on Blacks in America and globally. With the exception of Elijah Muhammad, Malcolm X, and the Nation of Islam (who followed Garvey's Blueprint) no person or movement has captured the Black male imagination like the Garvey Movement.

I see MLK and Huey P. Newton as political revolutionaries whose focus was the legal standing of Blacks within the empire; whereas the U.N.I.A. Movement transcended the law and white America. Marcus Garvey not only gave us moral, ethical, and economic philosophy, but forced us to see ourselves as the worldwide nation we truly are; He reminded us we were a global community that must assert itself on the international stage. Garvey was not an ideas man, but a man of logistics. His ideas were not to be pondered as theory but acted upon immediately with full strategy and determination. Wherever they were, Blacks were to engage in international trade, communication, and organization with each other and other "races." The Black Diaspora is not the sad byproduct of industrial slavery; but an opportunity for Black political, cultural, and economic tentacles to stretch around the globe.

His ideas are still inspiring Blacks worldwide, one hundred years later. The blueprint for success has been devised; it is now for us to follow the plan. Unfortunately, many are too slow to move and take positive leadership roles on the communal level. As far as I know Garvey was the first leader whose plan for Black self-determination centered on international trade and commerce; the UNIA not only established contacts in different countries but managed to buy ships so that we could truly move independently as merchants.

This was being done while Garvey was trying to establish a beachhead colony in Africa where an embryonic Black government could command from. Whatever is said about Garvey's flaws he cannot be accused of thinking small. His gaze was also focused on the mental health of the Black community, he was the first to seriously criticize the color divide among Blacks (light skinned vs. dark skinned / educated vs. uneducated) and broach the subject of "Black hair." He criticized those who advocated hair straightening or rejected the idea of natural Black beauty. Garvey also gave us the flag that we rally around when we are distressed, and need to symbolize solidarity.

There is no person (Black or white) that does not know that a Red, Black, and Green flag is a Black flag. When it is raised it means that "Black people" are mad. In fact all Black nationalist philosophy of substantive importance and cultural relevance can be traced back to Garvey / and Booker T Washington. While native born Black leadership was busy cultivating a Black man that would live in a white man's world, Garvey was cultivating Black men who would live successfully in a Black man's world.

This amalgam of foreign and native born Black creativity can be found in the literary movement of the Harlem Renaissance. Which included  writers, intellectuals and activist  from the Caribbean. In more recent history those contributing to Black culture hail from all parts of the world. The most influential Black man in the area of ancient Black history is Cheikh Anta Diop 1923-1986; a Senegalese born French trained Scientist/Anthropologist/ Philosopher/ Historian and Egyptologist. Diop has no equal in terms of his influence on  the Black historians and Pan African philosophy; Black historians hail him as "the last Pharaoh." One will be hard pressed to find a serious book written by Black scholars discussing African civilization without mention of Diop in their bibliography.

Furthermore, the American University system is host to many foreign born Black students who are in many respects benefiting from (affirmative action) hard fought Civil Rights battles that were won in the 60s and 70s. Consequently, there is no way to truly appreciate the phenomenon of Obama the self described "Black man" or the Obama family without embracing a Pan Africanist world view because he does not come from slave blood but yet we embrace him and his family as our own - because they are.

# THE LOGIC OF PAN AFRICANISM

Pan Africanism says that Black people are one people, no matter where they are. It is a philosophical posture that is both political and spiritual in nature. The spiritual aspect recognizes Blacks everywhere in the world, no matter their ethnicity or culture, as being different branches torn from the same tree. Being such they share the same ancient roots (genetic and cultural) which makes them kin with all the rights and obligations that comes with family.

The political aspect of Pan Africanism conveys the truth that, within the last 500 years, Blacks from Africa and the Diaspora have faced a common enemy in white supremacy. An enemy who has offered one of three options to every Black nation, clan, village, and individual they encounter: *submit to economic exploitation, cultural annihilation and global second class (third world) citizenship wherever you maybe found.* In the end Pan Africanism says Black people have common interest even if only for the sake of survival. It is not a ideology rooted in Black separatism, nor does it advocate prejudice of any kind. Pan Africanism is essentially a world view that if implemented, enthusiastically by Blacks, will turn into a system for cooperation, net working, and commercial synergy.

## SOCIAL TRUTH OF OUR UNITY

Reflecting on the people and neighborhoods I have known, and even within my own family I knew that we were already marrying and having children across ethnicities. When my sister bought her Nigerian boy friend home to our grandmother  nobody made any fuss over it (my sister actually looked more like his family than ours). And when they had a baby girl together there was nothing special about it. As an young adult I was surprised to discover so many Black families in my neighborhood, that I knew for years, had Hispanic last names and roots. Being in prison and taking stock of the Black population I came to realize the actual range and depth of our diversity. The males I meet are first, second, and third generation descendants of Haitians, Jamaicans, Dominicans, Puerto Ricans, Africans (from many countries), and many more lesser known countries.

Many are bi-lingual, most of them speak perfect English without accent, and if not informed of their genealogy it would be impossible to know their place of origin. Most of the guys I encounter that are second generation immigrants are assimilated culturally with native Blacks to the point of there being no distinction. Most have little contact or connection to the traditions, customs or people of their parent and grandparents. In fact they are often eager to assimilate into the larger Black culture (or at least blend seamlessly) because as children the stigma of being seen as African, Haitian, Jamaican or other  can be more difficult than plain old 'Black.' Even Jamaicans who have a  very proud,  energetic and magnetic culture are absorbed into the larger Black culture within a couple of generations. I point this out because the story of our origins is told in a simplified way; in  bits and pieces  or mere fragments of truth. I believe we are isolated from our larger narrative and stripped of context and facts. We are historically divided and conquered. If the story of the Black Diaspora is not told then the story of Black people is incomplete. Imagine telling the story of America without telling the English, Dutch, Germen, Irish, Scottish, Jewish, and Italian perspectives.

                                              BOB MARLEY (1980)


As it stands the genetic composition of most Blacks in America is undoubtedly of predominant  African stock. Even with centuries of rape and interracial unions we have retained our diverse good looks, rhythm, spirit, and  style. A few (measly) hundred years of bondage could not erase  ten thousand years of civilization imbedded into the fabric of the African soul. The buildings may crumble, families may break apart, and people may scatter and wander but the social, intellectual and genetic refinement could not be taken from us. I do not believe thoroughly civilized people can be reduced to the level of beasts; they can be turned into slaves very easily, but reducing them to savages or humans without dignity is next to impossible.

Many of us still know the religions of old and the names of god - and how to communicate with the Most High. Some had to go back and retrieve the rituals while others never lost them. Others hid them in plain sight; yet others  hid them from themselves. Many more have forgot the origin of that  which they have. In any case, when we dance and sing it all comes back- when we mourn it all appears.

Fat Black women look the same no matter the country they are born and language they speak. They are the foundation of the Black village, community, and hood, no matter where they are at. They are always feared and respected  divas. Like god they create something from nothing, their milk is the life blood and without them there would be no religion. They are always spiritual, sexual, and masculine. They are always subtle, clever, and control  their families with looks, whispers, grunts, and silence. Their zombie-like trances are the same no matter the name of the deity they pray  to. They are the most religious but the most practical. The proof of our unity is found in the ways of our mothers.

The last 500 years of History has produced a group of people who are ethnically and  visibly diverse and aware of their genetic complexity, even when they are in denial of it. A Pan Africanist perspective to geopolitics is our only logical path, it is the only way to reconcile the diversity already present in our homes and communities. We must feel comfortable in a world of many tongues and dialects; we must be at ease around  different shades, shapes,  and accents. We must come to  know different customs, manners, and styles of thinking and expression. Our taste must adapt to new foods, spices, and flavors. We must see ourselves in different lands under different flags doing different things.  Our land is wherever we happen to be, and we happen to be everywhere.  However,  before we can do this, we must first conceptualize  ourselves as part of a greater Black whole and then materialize it through action.

## CULTURAL TENSION

It is necessary to say these things because I am aware of the tension and cultural divide that plagues Black people in America. It is an insult to call a native born Black "a Jamaican" or to call a Jamaican a "Haitian" or to call a Haitian an "African" or to ask a dark skinned Dominican: 'What are you?' I see how people's native tongues are mocked and ridiculed and use to segregate them. And how groups isolate themselves and feel abused or under threat because they are different. In my youth  we  had 'beefs' with Jamaicans over control of neighborhoods; the same thing  was  taking place in Philadelphia.

Whether  its  Haitians,  Africans,  or  Jamaicans,  these scenarios play out wherever different tongues occupy the same space. Such tensions have generational consequences.  I have spoken to enough foreign born Blacks who express hurt at not being accepted into the fold  by 'American' Blacks. It causes them to be defensive and even more patriotic to their own flags and culture, or to hide their roots through assimilation; some even resort to shunning their mother tongue and heritage. In prison I noticed many who were reluctant to mention their ethnic roots.

They are masters at concealing their family's accent, they rarely speak cultural patois, out of fear of being identified as 'one of them;' a shame they learned growing up around other children, who are unforgiving in their treatment of those who are different. Sadly, for children and adults the word "dirty" is the preferred prefix when referring to outsiders, or when people of foreign nationality are mentioned. Childhood differences follow many into adulthood and influence the quality of relationship foreign  and native born Blacks are able to have.

It is also not lost on Native Blacks that foreign born Blacks arrive with or soon acquire prejudices of their own. Blacks born in America are perceived to be lower and less refined  or even too mixed (too much white in blood).  A favorite comment about  African Americans  is: 'they have no culture.' Adding to the absurdity is that whites often feel more at ease around Blacks with accents than they do African Americans. And will  express such ideas.

*A Congolese immigrant whom I met in the course of researching my book told me about the African Americans she knows at the supermarket where she works. "We are really different," she said about her community, as opposed to African Americans. "They don't have African values to be Black. "I asked her what that means. "To be black," she explained, "means you get married and you don't have children before." [she went on to say] "they ask you if you want marijuana. It's just normal for them. It's easy for them to say that "My ancestors were oppressed."6*

SUKETU MEHTA (Indian American)


Its fine if foreign born Blacks  think they  know America better than her own spawn. In any case, this constant arrival of outside Black culture and blood is a good thing for African Americans who in some cases have grown complacent, and stagnant.

We have to constantly replenish and reinvigorate the ranks because too many have been ground down by the empire and lost faith in themselves; drugs, welfare, alcoholism, and single parent homes are the bane of our existence. Foreign born Blacks arrive with a special zeal, and  generally don't  suffer from the same generational 'black clouds' that burden many urban families. They also often maintain healthy components of culture that have been lost to African Americans (like having many children and close-knit extended families) and  the old-world conservative values, lost to the generations of urbanized survivors of the war on drugs and  family breakdown.

Blacks of all backgrounds are coming together whether through cultural assimilation or sexual unions; we are in the process of reconstituting and becoming one diverse tribe. American psychology does not permit categories of Black or White and has a way of pushing people together and pulling others apart based on a color system. Only time will reveal the true nature of class and caste in America. When Black men and women are victimized and  abused by the state  (police) and its civilian counter parts, those who think they are different will realize their ethnic origins has no relevance here. And that color, unfortunately, is the common denominator between "us and them."

When America lays bare  other insidious manifestations of racial injustice, those who think they have transcend Blackness will be humbled. They will know that they are not in Kansas anymore (or they *are* in Kansas) and just how precarious their situation is. We will continue to march and protest for everybody whether they are grateful or not. At any rate, when it is time to vote, rally, march, protest, or burn to insist that "Black Lives Matter" it will be done under a Red, Black, and Green flag. In a sea of colorful  yellow, brown, and black and white faces.

# SECTION II

# SO MUCH SHAME

# MANY SHADES OF

# VICTIMOLOGY & METHODS OF

# COPING

Even before I began to take writing seriously I first spent many years attempting to understand the  thinking of humanity in general and of Black men in particular.  I was trying to discover why so many of the men where I am from fail in life; why they continued to go in and out of prison; and why they could not get their act together, even when there were no visible barriers blocking them. I quickly came to observe that in America Blacks have developed a very deep and profound victim complex; which is accompanied by many forms of shame.  This has been written about  by others and is well-known among those who treat African Americans on the psychiatric level.

Here,  I am attempting to articulate, in my own words, the nature of the victim's mind and thought pattern that I most frequently encounter among the men and women that I have come across in my experience. The central purpose of my books is to explore the mind and culture of the urban male and critique it with honesty. Not only did I want to write about the flawed thinking, I wanted to offer solutions where I felt they were necessary. As such, I have taken my time to listen to Black males and realized that in order to understand him it is essential to listen to him when he thinks no one is paying attention; it is here, in this space, that he most often reveals his inner most thoughts.

As it pertains to my examination of the male and his perception of himself and Black people I have discovered the following episodes in the Black experience weigh heavy on the soul and contribute to an unshakable  victimology that pervades our psychology:


**Being torn from our native soil turned into slaves;**

**The success of the plantation system at erasing thousands of year's worth of knowledge from our memories;**

**Constantly being reminded by ourselves and others of our past status as slaves, victims of white violence,  humiliation, and rape;**

**Our collective traumatic experience under Jim Crow and the urban police state;**

**The sabotage of the Black community by the White majority;**

**The manufactured ignorance and  poverty imposed on us.**

As a result of these acts of violence and manipulation that have persisted for centuries profound alienation has set into the culture and have given birth to many forms of shame. There is the shame of feeling lost and cut off from something larger; a shame of being too light or of being too dark; the shame of poverty while being surrounded by images of opulence; the shame of ignorance, while living in a world full of unlimited knowledge; the shame of being shackled by hopelessness and  dysfunction, while surrounded by people who are organized, efficient and disciplined; the shame of seeming powerless to prevent the many forms of attack and hostility coming from enemies; and the shame of  being a well-known historical victim who has never gotten his revenge.

In order to learn about '*the souls of black folk*' *a* person has to listen to people when they are vulnerable and become skilled at interpreting  their songs, cries, and lamentations. It is here at this sad place where you will hear the truth and come to know what keeps us chained to the past. The further we go back in time and  closer to slavery we get, we find generations not far removed from plantation life or Jim crow sharecropping were reluctant to discuss their past. Their pain was  fresh, it was not something to be worn on the sleeve or used as a crutch; it was something to be buried deep in the depths of the mind, and blocked by a thousand psychological tricks. Whether it was through liquor, music, or religion the traumatic experience was to be forgotten, it was to be overcome by any means necessary.

I once said to my grandmother who was born in 1925: "*I am trying to figure out where we come from.*" She, without pause, retorted: "*I'm trying to forget.*" I have discussed this  with others, and they agree with my observation. The  older generations avoid, at all cost, discussions of what they had seen and experienced - to the point of refusing to acknowledge their pain. However, these were the old ways; if people in the past saw little meaning in speaking of their victimization it is  simply not the case today. Today people revel in their victim status, they wear it openly, and they want to be acknowledged as someone that something happened to and they want to broadcast the pain to whoever will listen. The pursuit of history and focus on one's own victimhood is actually a modern luxury that has turned into a fixation.

For too many our history, particularly the victimization of our bodies, has become the defining feature of our cultural narrative. Black victimization has become similar to  holocaust mania and the Native American trail of tears elegy. These very painful episodes in the history of these groups has sadly come to define them in the minds of many; they are people who are being remembered by what others have done to them and nothing more. Native American and Jewish, in the imagination of others, has  come to represent sadness and victim. They are becoming known and defined, first and foremost, by the genocide committed against them. I believe that based on our resemblance to other victimized groups,  in focusing considerable cultural energy to the subjects of slavery and oppression, that a dangerous cult of victimology has developed and now permeates every strata and class of Black culture.

# WHAT IS VICTIMOLOGY?

Victimology is when people profess, or has (intellectually and conceptual) internalized present and future limitations on themselves. Especially in terms of their (individual and collective group) abilities/ capabilities; based on past (historic status) limitations or obstacles real or perceived.

Victimology is believing and accepting that something cannot or should not be done (as a custom) based upon one's true or false perception of a historic inability to do that thing.

Victimology is the pervasive subconscious doubt about one's own ability that underpins a person's worldview.

Victimology is expressed in the belief that the low station in life that one was born into is both natural and destined; therefore irresistible.

Victimology is the internalized belief that effort is futile because others have monopolized all the opportunities; and you are being held back because everyone is colluding against you.

Victimology is feeling self-righteous and believing you are morally better than your 'oppressor' because you are a victim and your enemy is an aggressor; and believing that he will get what's coming to him (in the afterlife or through karma) because god and the universe demands it.

Victimology is absolving yourself (the victim) of responsibility to act or  resist oppression because god will get even or karma will intervene.

Victimology is the belief that one is absolved from  personal responsibility to do what they know is right because they were not given what they perceive as an even hand in life.

Victimology is the belief that no matter what you do  the system is going to win. The belief that the powers aligned against you (real or imagined) are destined to prevail so resistance is ultimately futile.

Victimology is looking for and expecting to be discriminated against, and looking forward to it so that it confirms the expectation that life is not fair.

Victimology is the belief that doing the right thing is not worth doing if there is too much personal sacrifice involved, because the chance of you altering the outcome is small and so the risk is not worth it.

Victimology is the belief that there is a certain behavior that Blacks must perform in order to qualify as Black.

Victimology is the belief that skin color is the sole determinant of one's future or citing one's skin color as a personal crutch and impediment to progress.

Victimology is the belief that the shade or hue of your skin is a cause for personal shame or personal pride.

Victimology is the belief that one's hair texture is inferior or superior while using European hair as the standard from which all hair is judged.

Victimology is the belief that all the power in the world has been obtained by Europeans and it is for them to divide it as they see fit.

Victimology is to believe in the negative stereotypes  cast against a racial or ethnic group.

Victimology is the belief that White people are inherently more competent than anybody else.

Victimology is the act of marrying or dating outside of one's race based on the belief that one is "progressing"  or moving up in status or believing that one is escaping the stigma of Blackness by doing so. And believing that  persons of your own race are inferior or not worthy of you.

Victimology is the act of blaming the system for your own moral, ethical, and intellectual failures.

Victimology is the act of teaching your children  all or any aspect of victimology.

Victimology goes mostly unexpressed and can be  difficult to detect in individuals who appear otherwise healthy and confident. Nevertheless, victimology rest on a foundation of confusion based on a fundamental misunderstanding of how the world works at its core. If you think like a victim you will move like a victim.  I can't say how many times I have heard the phrase: "They won't let us do that." This statement surfaces every time  someone suggests a plausible course of action to confront some economic, political, or social dilemma.  I once suggested that we as Black merchants begin  importing our goods from other countries to circumvent the foreign middlemen that have a grip on the inner city retail markets. The first thing that exited the mouth of the council of males I was addressing was: "They won't let us do that." I asked them: 'Who is they?'  Then I pointed out that Black people and many others are doing this very thing every single day and have been for decades.

This sort of doubt is common among the poor and when they are met with facts they usually fall into a state of silence or confusion. Sometimes they look off into the distance, other times they look at me baffled as if I shattered their beautiful victim narrative. Which has supported them in their disbelief in themselves.

After many of these kinds of exchanges it did not take me long to realized that class, station or status determined a person's understanding of how the world actually works.  In general, the higher a person's  status was the more informed they were, and the more detailed knowledge they  possessed about the nature and mechanics of society. I also discovered that there is a willful incompetence and lethargy that accompanies being a victim, wherein some people prefer not to know things that conflict with or disturb their beliefs.

I concluded that many people cannot gather the energy to resist their situation because to resist victimhood is in actuality resisting their own will to disbelieve in themselves. The defeated victim is complacent,  he or she  is able to carry out monotonous routines because their  mind need not exert itself. However, learning new information and application of new techniques for distant rewards seems pointless.

The victim will justify their lack of effort by claiming  that invisible forces will not allow them to ascend the ladder of success or obtain power. They often cite the dangers involved in having ambitious aspirations, even pertaining to lawful endeavors. This is evidence that fear and confusion are pillars of victimhood. The very real barriers caused by gender, class and  racism pale in comparison to the power of the mind's prison, which prevents dreams and imagination from entering or escaping. The victimized mind does not say to itself: *'let me investigate this thing so that I may find a way around that problem, or change the way things are done; let me challenge, change or otherwise resist.'* Instead it resigns itself to defeat by invoking, *'they won't let us do that;'* This is the same  mantra that has been passed down through the ages from slave to slave, fed to babies through breast milk, and whispered into the ears of children while they sleep.

Projects that require a little tenacity but are otherwise easy to initiate seem like extraordinary feats in the mind of the victim. It would not matter if you gave them a hand-held supercomputer with access to global intelligence and limitless capabilities. They will just use it to play games and take cute pictures of themselves,  or use it to gossip and cause remote mayhem. With all the information and potential power on the earth in the palm of their hand  they will say 'its not enough.'

Victimology is not limited to the  least educated in our society, it can and does affect all classes. It is important to note that victimology is used strategically as a political weapon by all political leadership to foment resentment  and hate of others  (especially against minorities). Leaders  constantly focus on minor, imagined, and exaggerated injuries committed against them, and  justify the subjugation, oppression, attack, murder, and genocide of  others.

This is currently deployed by the America's right wing political establishment and has been the case for over a century. A large percentage of white men in America feel (has been indoctrinated to believe) they have been wronged by the U.S. government and all of her minority conspirators; and that it is his duty to act in some capacity (through the bullet or the ballet) to prevent further victimization. It should be noted that both Hitler and Osama Bin Laden believed they were victims and their wars were launched with the idea of revenge in mind.

I highlight this to demonstrate that victimology has different expressions under different conditions or leadership; and it can be used to both paralyze or to inspire. I am convinced that Black people are overwhelmingly under the spell of a paralyzing species of victimology. The symptoms of which are pessimism, lethargy, cynicism, depression, confusion, denial,  hopelessness, frustration, stress, apathy, and self-hate. This is not always the case, now and then victimology inspires people to resist their historic aggressors.

That said, I conclude that there are two strains of victimology; I will call them **defeatism victimology** (mostly described  above)  and  **resistance  victimology.**  Resistance victimology, on the contrary,  is invigorating to the human soul; it gives birth to  innovations,  creativity,  and  clarity of  purpose.

**Resistance victimology** thrives in desperation and determination to overcome life or death obstacles; all physical borders, imaginary boundaries, and perceptual limitations are ignored; only  two things remain - here and there.

It is my belief that many Black and white intellectuals place considerable focus on our oppressive condition because they believe that it will lead to enlightenment, and inspire the masses to resist their condition. These sort of thinkers believe we will become radically activated  by tales of humiliation and struggle. They believe that Blacks will get bit with the  bug of **resistance victimology**, but there is a fatal flaw in their logic. They assume that everyone will respond to the information the same way - by reaching a determination to take up revolution – when this is far from the case. History is powerful and  does  often  inspire  people  to  take  up  a  cause  they  think  is righteous, however, everyone cannot be fed the same diet. The same story that inspires people to take up arms can cause others to bury their heads in the sand.

In addition, there are other responses that may arise when such negative ideas and images are introduced to the mind; notably depression, hostility, and apathy. This would explain the well-known aversion  to  (Black)  history  found  among  both  the  educated  and uneducated African Americans. If learning  history only resulted in Black people being inspired why do they so often turn away from it? If reading about their history gave them confidence, self-respect, and positive affirmation history books would be flying off the shelves.

The men that I encounter are overwhelmingly under the spell of defeatism victimology. Black people in general are under the spell of defeatism victimology. Examples of this are many, but I will cite  a few. During Obama's 2008 run for the Presidency there were Black authors writing books, articles and making their  media circuits on "*why Obama could not win*;" and citing every reason under the sun why victory was impossible. One even claimed that Obama could not win because Michelle  Obama was too dark. Many  of whom would be considered intelligent by any standard, but these men were consumed by a defeatist mindset.  These people did not hate Obama they just did not believe in him or in the potential for America to allow someone like him (like themselves) to elevate to the station of presidency.

On a side  note after Obama won the presidency many Black males in prison were overwhelmed with celebration, but there were others who booed over Obama's success. This was not a subset of Black republican prisoners, nonetheless, they were audibly disappointed. I interpreted their disappointment  over Obama's win as being an attack on their victim status; Obama's win contradicted the Black belief that white America would not allow Blacks to reach the highest political offices in the nation. And this contradiction went against everything they had been led to believe and wanted to believe - for this they were upset. I have come to understand that some Blacks do not want to give up their victim status and will defend their right to be  victims to the death. With the loss of their historic victim status comes the loss of  their Black identity.

It is well known that many of the Civil rights gains were achieved while <u>most</u> Blacks did not take active part in the movement, and even resisted the message of the movement. Some had to be forced and coerced  into cooperation. The Southern boycotting movement of the 1950s and 1960s was not an entirely voluntary protest, Blacks had to be constantly pressured by their leaders to hold the line. What we see today as a voluntary Civil rights struggle for Black liberation was actually a movement that had to drag many of the rank and file kicking and screaming into freedom. Because mythology has been allowed to replace truth, those who did not want to buck or resist the system out of fear, are forever unknown.

Today everyone looks like a hero when at the time they would rather have remained victims of the  system than risk their lives, jobs, and privileges for future freedom.  We have no way of knowing the true scale of the sacrifice made by the men and women who risked it all so their children could be free. Based on historical precedents going back to the plantation system I believe the first order of any social-movement organization is to realize that all Black people are not coming along with the struggle for equality. Moreover, some may even pose the greatest threat and obstacle to progress.

# MANY SHADES OF COPING AS A VICTIM

There are many shades of coping when one has an aversion to a particular sort of victim-narrative of history. Here are some of the worst manifestations:

- Turning completely away from the past, by rejecting it as irrelevant.

- Living in denial of history by refusing to believe that certain things ever happened, continue to happen, or that there is not a lasting legacy still in place, based on these historic relationships.

- Not wanting to identify racially or ethnically with fellow victims, and opening the door for unconscious identification with ones oppressor – physically, behaviorally, and rationally.

Developing the following behavioral traits:

- Developing deep animus toward their own skin and anything linked to it including that which is considered "Black culture," including music, dress, speech patterns, and behavioral norms, to the point of not wanting to be associated with anything perceived as 'Black;' which can include dating partners or spouses.

- Bleaching of the skin going out of the way to erase all traces of Blackness and engaging in plastic surgeries to wipe away African noses to replace them with aquiline monstrosities.

- Altering the eye color (of their iris with contacts and other cosmetic practices) spending huge sums  on synthetic or organic hair to achieve European aesthetic.

- Engage in the abuse of Black people whenever there is the ability to exercise power over them,  and to distance themselves from Blacks, or critique them,  based on perceived physical or cultural flaws and humiliate and/ or oppress them.

- Insubordination to Black people in authority out of the internal belief that they are inherently unfit for positions of power, and should be disqualified  from holding real status.

- To be severely defensive and have an unhealthy neurotic concern of what white people think of them.

- Losing oneself in religious devotion to scripture where one disappears into the contemplation of the next life, and searching for meaning by interpreting all phenomenon through the nebulous and mysterious words of men  dead for thousands of years.

The greatest battlefield of Black people worldwide is not the physical territory which we have to defend, nor is it our bodies which may suffer abuse and decay. The toughest terrain that we must fight over is the landscapes of our minds. In terms of coping with victimhood, a person's worldview, or what can loosely be called "ideology" or beliefs system,  is the most difficult architecture to dismantle.

In America, Eurocentric logic is deeply rooted into the bedrock of the  national culture. It has been the foundation of mainstream thinking for centuries. Through history, literature, law, philosophy, popular media, business, science, entertainment, and academia the

Eurocentric worldview and aesthetic have saturated our psyche. It is almost impossible not to be contaminated by this mind-set. Only through rigorous self-inspection and ideological purging (and replacement) can a person overcome such thinking. The most dangerous type of victim are those who have surrendered and accepted the very ideas that keep them in bondage. They are dangerous because they do not appear racially hostile, but internally they are completely compromised philosophically,  spiritually, intellectually, and emotionally.

Among their constituents we find many who claim to be "Republicans or Conservatives." These Blacks often sincerely align themselves philosophically with people who are openly and secretly hostile to our pursuit of power; and whose 'golden age' is a time when We existed as sharecropping serfs. The same people  eager to strip us of hard-fought political gains. I have never understood how Black 'Republicans' or 'Conservatives' are able to ignore or tolerate the open white nationalism associated with the GOP's 'big tent'. More so today, when the party has grown very intolerant, and those who do not conform to its narrow agenda are ostracized.

A point of clarification is needed here. Many of our greatest leaders were rather conservative men and women (in values) who negotiated with all sorts of men in order to achieve political ends. That said, our leaders could distinguish between their values and their intimate affiliations. They did not try to defend people who were openly hostile to our progress. Unlike some today who call themselves 'Black conservatives' and take on these identities with militancy.

Let's be clear I have many ideas that run parallel with some right-wing factions, e.g. gun rights, low taxes, religious freedom, just to name a few. And if it came down to it I could vote for a republican on matters where I felt my interest were being served, but that does not make me one of them. I am not so emotionally or intellectually tied to any political party as to make me 'one of them.' Especially those who walk hand in hand with people who believe they are my superiors. I see Black Republicans as those who have accepted the current power dynamic and wish to put a façade of respectability and dignity on their submission.

Yet there are others who immerse themselves in the victim-narrative and wear it like a costume. Slavery and its sociological repercussions are among their favorite topics of discussion; they are consumed by the question of *"what they did to us"* and are constantly on the lookout for "micro-aggressions" of every sort. Not only do they see a racist around every corner, they *must* point them out with vehement indignity - as if a snake had slithered into a tea party. They see racists everywhere, whether they are there or not. They need to see them and want to see them, in order to validate their expectations as a victim. For them everything, no matter how trivial, is "racist." It is not uncommon for them to inflate their hardships and suffering until it is equal to slaves or negroes in the Jim Crow south. *"Man, we got it worse than them, this shit is just like slavery, ain't nothing changed."*

I have heard this sort of blasphemy uttered more than once, and the sentiment is not uncommon among poorly educated minds, who do not understand the books they have read. Neither do they realize the depth from which we have risen mentally, and economically. Too many have a perverse interpretation of our history, and never really grasp the complexity of the Black experience. They forgot or never knew the most important aspect of Black culture is that: *we are now, and have always been, more than victims*. Prior to slavery, during slavery, after slavery, and in this moment, our story has *always* been about more than victimhood; and we have never defined ourselves by what was done to us.

There are many ways for individuals to cope with internalized victimhood, these are but a few of the most acute manifestations of victimology. These are in no way coping mechanisms exclusive to Blacks; they can be found across cultures and continents wherever there exists an oppressor/victim dynamic. All of the behaviors outlined are used to cope with a wide range of emotional disorders not necessarily limited to the feeling of victimization.

## VICTIMS AVOID RESPONSIBILITY

Many males I encounter cannot imagine themselves or Black people as anything other than victims; this is who and what they understand Black people to be - besides gangsters, pimps, sports figures, and rappers. For many, especially the least educated, responsibility - a condition of power - is something we cannot have. It conflicts with their worldview. Responsibility is for those with power- and that is something we simply don't have. Many don't want to entertain  the idea that  despite our collective past we still have duties and responsibilities - to each other, our families, and to the broader community. They don't want to be confronted with the fact that we must be the ones to repair our  neighborhoods by setting a higher standard for ourselves.

The roles we play in our own genocide is a taboo conversation. Facing the truth about the crisis of absent fathers from their children's lives and the fact that we are helping to perpetuate these cycles of poverty is off the table. Bringing up the need to question regressive aspects of our culture, as well as confront 'the system'  may get you dirty looks or dismissed. They don't want to hear this part of the story. They have to be the victim, nothing will shake this premise.  That is absolute and final.

Many fail to realize that they have already lost. Sitting around talking or thinking about what white people did to us, out of resentment, is a waste of  time.  This does not mean we do not feel anger and  pain at the crimes committed against us, or seek retribution in some form or another. It means we are not delving into these books and consuming other forms of media exclusively to inflict pain on ourselves out of self-pity; or to feel self-righteousness because we have suffered. Being a victim can become a warm blanket, and provide the perfect cover for failing  to take bold action when the opportunity exits.

...and talking about what they did to us is dumb,
what we need to be talkin about is, what we gonna do to them...7

ONYX/2 Wrongs

# SPREADING VICTIM HOOD THROUGHOUT THE COMMUNITY

Nonstop discussions of slavery, Jim Crow, and the Black experience can be found on the lips of people from every class. Still, a majority of Black people do not spend their mental energies thinking about our past oppression - some even refuse to acknowledge it all together. However, the subject of our victimization is enough of a presence in academia, cinema, TV, literature, and pop culture and music to have made a negative impression on the minds of the masses.

We must find a pedagogical way to transmit our history without indoctrinating our people with a sense of victimhood. We do not need to teach children they are victims in order to teach them Black history. There are many ways to teach the "Black experience" without instilling fear, self-loathing, or trauma. If our story cannot be taught without inflicting trauma on our collective psyche then we must consider whether our story is worth telling at all; Or if our history should only be taught to those who are seeking it. We must also consider whether the teaching of Black history should be entrusted to a specialized class of modern intellectual griots, in order for them to preserve and skillfully transmit stories that are too depressing for children and adults to bear witness to.

The authors of books, articles, and academic research papers are well meaning; as are journalists chronicling contemporary Black subject matter, and the makers of documentary or cinematic films with Black life or tragedy as the theme. They do not set out to diminish Black self-esteem or add to our depression. Nonetheless, the way in which our history is being sold, told, and depicted is having unintended consequences, a large segment of Black America is repulsed by what they see, hear, or read about themselves, and this cuts across generations.

This is not a phenomenon unique to African Americans it is a common phenomenon found in populations that have had traumatic experience. Author Walter Kaufmann cites philosopher Friedrich Nietzsche as saying: "*the unhistorical [forgetting the past] and the historical [remembering the past] are equally needed for the health of an individual, a people, and a culture.*"8 In *The Birth of Tragedy*, Nietzsche emphasized the horrors of history as a challenge that may lead the weak to negate life, while it leads the strong to create the beautiful.9

It is clear that Nietzsche considered the study or contemplation of history as potentially detrimental, especially for "the weak," or those who could not overcome the potential depression that goes hand and hand with recalling painful events. In the Black community there is antipathy over history books, slave movies, maid movies, and cinema that depicts Blacks in servile positions. *"I'm tired of this stuff, I ain't looking at that,"* is heard common enough by the old and the young. They instinctively know any mention of 'history' inevitably leads back to the plantation and will encompass rape, pain, lynching, bowing, and sambo-like groveling; conjuring feelings of powerlessness. In the mainstream telling of our history we never seem to win a battle, who can blame anybody for refusing to listen to our elegy, which often sounds like a eulogy.

The watered down presentation of Harriet Tubman, Frederick Douglass, and Sojourner Truth actually repulses (and it should) any well-adjusted adolescent who senses that something is amiss in these dark fairytales. It is just as difficult getting through the civil rights era folklore about MLK, Rosa Parks, dogs, hoses, and sticks without experiencing despair. Some of the imagery is beyond horrifying, even for a  mature adult. There is no way to quantify the harm done to an individual psyche let alone a collective one after being constantly bombarded with such negative images throughout your entire life (ad infinitum). What child or adult could come away from it without developing hate or fear of white people because of what they have done? But hating white people is certainly bad and maybe illegal, and so  they settle for hating themselves instead, which is perfectly fine.

Contrary to belief, Black people don't hate Black history, what they are hostile to is to negative depictions of themselves. Instead of depressing themselves by reading about their oppression they turn away from it entirely. I have seen faces of people light up, there postures change, and pride emanate from them after having read stories of Africans fighting against European colonialism, Caribbean slave revolts,  Southern Blacks resisting white oppression, and Black success stories. When young men and women see that once-upon-a-time (in pre-colonial Africa) Africans had organized militaries, prosperous cities, and lived by unmatched moral law they can't believe it, and are in awe. The same can be said of Black triumph stories in America or elsewhere. Young men have outright told me, *"Man,  you got to let people know about this, if I would have known about this I would have never got into this gang or turned to crime."* This is further proof that they themselves see their current condition as a consequence of  historical circumstances.

On the other hand, a mind that has consumed nothing but victim narratives is a dangerous place. A male once told me: "America  was the white man's land that he had made for himself and Martin Luther King Jr. was basically asking the white man for some of his land. And that was the legacy set in place since the Civil Right era." It's one thing for a fool to blurt things out without understanding,  but this male actually believed he was informed and therefore ranks as something much worse than a fool. It was not my first time hearing this statement, or debating this point with people who were even brighter; I was, therefore, versed in the Black rationale behind this declaration.  I had to correct him, and  explained to him that there were many flaws in his argument.

The first of which was the fact that he had accepted the white supremacist version of  historical truth,  and in doing so he doomed himself.  I disagree with the entire premise of the argument, that "this is the white man's land," therefore everything derived from that logic is  untrue. This is not the "white man's land" this is a land full of white men.  This country and its land has always and will always be by ruled by those who  can  manage to control it. Martin Luther King Jr. was not asking the white man for his rights. Martin Luther King was telling the white man:

*This land is also ours by law (laws put in place by your forbearers),  we have been here hundreds of years, (longer than many of you) we pay taxes, we are drafted into war, we are entitled to share in the bounties and freedoms;  yes you white man have been able to subjugate us for a very long time due to your numeric superiority and violence,  but that was then and this is now. We Blacks are spread out across this country we are vast in number and many of us are fed up and want a fight, no matter the outcome.  I do not want that, I want to resolve our problems not by violence but by  non-violent political  means,  if that is possible - and I believe that it is possible. I am running out of time I cannot hold back the masses of frustrated Blacks and whites who are on the verge of  rebellion.  You must reform the political machinery for the better or there will be no peace in this land. We are not going anywhere, we are here to stay whether the worst of you accept that or not.  And for you Blacks who want to rebel  (and whites who want the status quo) I warn you that this will be bloody and I do not believe that this is in our interest as a people and country.*

MLK was presenting an ultimatum in the best language he knew how- the prophetic warning of the holy man.  MLK was not begging the white man for his land, he was fighting with spirit the of god for rights that had been afforded to us. Rights that were afforded to us post American revolution by the various state governments and by federal legislators after Civil war. White people know that because of the historic nature of this country's existence, this is not their land and that their grip on power is not absolute; this is the reason they are so politically insecure. This country belongs to whoever is in the best position to manage it.

Think about it, do all of the Mexicans, Guatemalans, Nicaraguans, Haitians, El Salvadorans, Venezuelans, Dominicans, Africans or Cubans flooding into America (legally or illegally) care that some white men believe this is their exclusive country? The answer is, No!

They only care about survival. Survival of their families, to be exact. People fleeing violence, poverty and hunger don't have the luxury to care about opinions. They come here with the same ambitions as the white man's ancestors; to live, work, prosper and build a foundation for their children. These people come to settle the land and carve out territory and space for themselves; their political ambition is inevitable.

What angry white people think becomes more irrelevant by the day; while they sit back counting their guns and bullets, their "replacements" keep quiet and count their babies. We will see whose country this is in 200 more years.

In truth, without this influx of foreign blood and labor the American economy would grind to a halt. The military would not be combat or logistically proficient; the tax base would be overburdened; prisons and hospitals would be dangerously understaffed; and farming and manufacturing would be in peril.

Legal and illegal immigrants are not being let into the country for their own sake, but for the sake of the country's stability and future vitality.

This is what I find so dangerous in accepting the white supremacist ideology. If a Black person actually believes this land is rightfully the white man's then it must be a serious psychological impediment to his internal motivation. If he believes he is living in a land that's not his own, and our people obtained what they did by begging he cannot be inspired to build anything of lasting substance; everyday he wakes up with a serious obstruction to his imagination. If he believes he is not legitimately entitled to a place on American soil then how can he fight for his place or his family's place within society? I don't think he can. How can he battle hostile forces with spiritual, moral, and intellectual firmness if he believes he is just begging? My question is how did we get here, how was this broken defeated man created, and what will it take to destroy this toxic mindset that plagues the Black male mind?

Let me be clear, I understand there is a very long tradition in America where, many if not most, white men believe and act like this is their country and theirs alone; I am simply stating that I don't care what they think, the facts on the ground will always dictate reality. And in life the facts are always changing, the Native Americans also thought this was their land and that private property was not a real thing; look at the reality of what they thought.

# LIMITED OPTIONS OF APPROACH

We are a people trying to shake off the dark cloud of the past, as such, we have very few options ahead of us. I conclude we have three choices before us. 1. The first is being Black and accepting the victim status and stigma that goes along with that past. 2. The second is to opt out and become free by disassociating our (individual) selves from our collective past - and the stain of color. This is done quite often by people who claim they are "not Black" or falsely trace (from delusion/ subconscious shame?) their roots to some exotic people and place. They may also link themselves with movements or isms (religions, philosophical, or political) ideologies who make a pretense of transcending race and nationality. 3. The third option is to reinvent ourselves by looking at our past experience from a different angle and telling a deeper story. One that begins long before slavery. A narrative with the goal of transmitting an optimistic future of infinite potentials; where we are taught that resistance, refinement, and cohesion are fundamental components to our survival. If this is the case, we have to embrace our past in bondage with new enthusiasm, either turning it into a point of pride or (at most) a minor footnote in our long human saga. This requires us to take hold of our narrative without fear and to tell it in a way that is healthy for the collective souls of Black folk. What is amazing about this whole idea of this glorious saga is that it is absolutely true, we only need to take hold of our story before it is corrupted by others.

Diop

74

# WHY IS THERE SO MUCH FOCUS ON OUR OPPRESSION?

Modern American literature and media are saturated with coverage of the "Black experience." There are many well written and researched books by Black, White and Jewish academics whose scholarship and data is beyond reproach and are important in documenting important episodes in Black history. Such literature is supported by an impressive industry of interviews, magazine articles, cinema, and documentaries; many of the topics are only recently getting the attention they deserve. Even so, writers and film makers obsessive focus on our oppressive past and present is hard to ignore. In addition, their analysis and conclusions are not inspiring or designed to motivate Blacks to take action or wake from our sleep.

I believe there is an (unhealthy) pathological concentration on slavery and victimization relative to more optimistic stories and portrayals of Black life. Black suffering is currently in style and favored at the expense of more positive coverage of our success. It seems that Black people (of academia) find it imperative to write books, articles, make films, and discuss (in open forums) the topic of suffering. They have cornered some niche market where liberal sympathy translates into Black victim dollars. This has resulted in the over production and glut of literature and cinema on victimization. Is it possible this is the only genre in which they can get attention? I find similar focus on Jewish Holocaust-centered cinema and literature. In both cases there seems to be a sort of victim-narrative mania.

Black artist and intellectuals have resorted to producing non-militant art and literature, and in doing so have gained access to 'establishment' media (major newspapers, magazines, and media outlets) where they make their book tours on television and talk radio. Where they receive all the positive book, film, and movie reviews needed to bolster their credentials and raise their academic or artistic profile. It is primarily through left leaning networks where they get their stamp of approval. It doesn't matter if the subject is school segregation, reparations, the one drop rule, the color caste in America, the prison industrial complex, gang violence, general murder, Black hair (nappy roots and all), colorism within Black America,  having the so-called "talk" with boys, wealth gaps, or up from the ghetto survival stories. These things are seen as authentically Black issues.

Tragedy is the only thing 90% of authors (novelists included), journalists, film makers and personalities (with mainstream attention) traffic in. They get recognition and compensated for speaking, writing, and documenting our misery in some form or another. If a Black person is not discussing some dismal aspect of 'Black life' they get little attention.  Issues that we have not ironed  out or even raised among each other (for serious discussion) are being presented to mostly academic audiences for their consumption, contemplation, and entertainment. Topics and critiques of Black and white America that were, until recently, only mentioned by the Black nationalist as an act of concern for the mental health and survival of the nation have now become mainstream matters for National Public Radio. The analysis of the white supremacist social order in front of a poor all Black room makes one a militant nationalist. However,  raising the same topics to a mostly white audience in a measured tone makes one a 'progressive.' As usual, truly radical authors and thinkers are never invited  to these venues.

# WHO IS BLACK HISTORY WRITTEN FOR?

I do not believe that a majority of the literature and documentary films being produced are actually created for Black consumption. African American, Jewish, and Anglo scholars author many good books that are well researched and sympathetic to the Black struggle for equality, but consistent with their academic origins we are objectified. These are books written about us, but not necessarily for us. I cannot count the number of times Prof. Henry Louis Gates Jr. has been on television discussing Black History, but (like clockwork) finds himself commenting on what white people used to say about Blacks on this particular subject. Whether the topic is Black intellectual achievement, Timbuktu, Christianity in Ethiopia, or more ancient civilizations.

Who gives a shit about what David Hume, Voltaire, or Hegel had to say! Our story for him and many more is never good enough to stand alone; it is always there to prove something to somebody - their true audience. To prove we ain't as stupid or as savage as they claimed. "Black history" for a certain class of men and women is used to prove that Black people are part of civilization. Gates is a Harvard Professor of "African" studies but his favorite discipline is the philosophy and critical opinions of dead white men.

This species of literature and entertainment has a long tradition in America, even the 'slave narratives' of the 18th and 19th century were not written for fellow slaves or free Blacks, but rather for white abolitionist. Apart for the newly freed man or woman having a chance to tell their story these books were meant to humanize those still in bondage. This body of literature was intended to inspire white philanthropist and Aid Societies to support and fund a righteous cause. In addition to persuade white citizens to be sympathetic to the plight of the oppressed African and turn away from their indifference to slavery. Which would eventually lead to passage of state laws abolishing slavery, in America and other countries. White authors also wrote books  in this genre. Harriet Beacher Stowe's *Uncle Tom's Cabin* is credited with stirring up white sympathy by her portrayals of enslaved men and women she knew.

These stories had to be pack full of gruesome details about oppression that would make their  patrons (who pay the bills) both weep and salivate. These writers (Black and White) also did national and international tours  to promote their books and tell their story. The production of this sort of literature and entertainment continued to the Harlem Renaissance where much of the books served similar end. The unstated aim of this literature was not lost on Black writers, who knew what their benefactors wanted to hear and adjusted the subject-matter accordingly. This literature is still being produced, but now for a modern consumer, who still wants to hear about the worst aspects of Black existence; the only difference is that Blacks themselves have forgotten the origins of this strain of literature and now also demand to hear and examine the worst aspects of our culture. This reminds me of the beginnings of gangster rap, when music artist and executives discovered that rappers could get controversial attention by abandoning political critiques of the system and  instead telling the worst aspect of their lives - even lying in order to seem more authentic. Young white suburban consumers drove up early demand for this genre, which had once been relegated to the a minor segment of hip hop scene. We now have an industry of music where everybody is  rewarded for  claiming to be a killer and drug dealer.

Just like early African American literature the art form of Rap has evolved, and with it the need to sustain its paying audience. Every rapper now claims to have been born in a trash can and had to claw their way to the top, on a pile of dead bodies. For shock value they weave dark lies into colorful tales, in order to appeal to a certain segment of the Hip hop consumers, who craved this sort of glimpse into the world of ghetto youth. I can't count the number of  times Jay-Z has been asked about his drug dealing past by white interviewers.

Like their earlier literary counterparts (of the 1920 and 1930s) rappers (in the 1980s & 1990s) complained about fellow artist making commercial music, which was considered 'selling out' or 'going pop.' This is what groups like EPMD meant by "the cross-over." Many well-known artist including Tupac Shakur tried to strike a balance between creating the music they wanted to make and the music they felt they had to make in order to get mainstream air play. It was not that the artist did not want to become famous or get monetary reward, they simply wanted these things while being true to themselves. These artist knew that once the music was made for the radio and the consumer its was no longer being made for the benefit of people, but only for a profit. And for a profit people will say and do anything, even  if it was detrimental to the people. The list of songs and rap artist who railed against "going pop" 'selling out" and going commercial is too extensive to cite, but such  thinking is a relic of a long-gone past. Commercial success is the goal of every rapper and they will say and do anything they need to achieve it.

This aspect of Hip hop culture is now driven by its own momentum, yet few remember its not so distant beginnings. Hip hop is not alone, Blues music, as a genre, was created by Black men and women who use this art form to express their frustration, sadness, and elegy;  their audience was primarily their own folk. Now the Blues caters to the expectations and tastes of its growing white audience, who  want to buy authentic pain and heartache. That being the case artist must manufacture and market their product and persona to appeal to this demographic. Does this pressure from commercial forces change how the music evolves, and if so, to what expense to the spirit of the people?

I believe Black culture continues to be driven by such forces; which is to say, our culture is being shaped by those who must tailor their politics, message, or art to accommodate (or be sensitive to) white patrons, whether they be individual consumers, corporations, or institutions who control the purse strings and access to social status. In such a case, no matter what it seems Black culture is neither independent nor organic, but the product of a complex form of manipulation, coercion, and duress at the stage of its creation and in its expression; I believe this is true whether it be writers, rappers, journalist, academics or educators.

What am I saying? I am arguing that much of mainstream "Black" literature, art, and entertainment (music included) are not authentic expressions of culture by Black artist, but the opposite. They are instead carefully constructed depictions of the "Black experience" meant to appeal to the taste and sentiments of diverse consumers; either as entertainment or political and intellectual voyeurism. Mainstream literature in particular is being produced to either make us look clean and civilized or to depict our misery born of desperation, caused by white oppression (to validate political objectives); or with commercial, and academic status as an objective in mind. None of which is produced to create militant minded men and women, the kind of people needed to overthrow this current paradigm, where we are at the bottom. Militant art whose critique is meant to inspire new generations is not being created, because white opinions or our (economic or social) relationship to them, is the driving factor of the art's creation. We are not contributing to the culture for the sake of our own legacy. Instead we are creating to be compensated, rewarded, or to look good for our intended audience.

If media outlets report on Black issues ears perk up when there is tragedy to report about. The stories are narrated as to convey Black victimization that can only be cured by the hope and resiliency of Black folk. Rarely is a story meant to inspire Black people into action on their own behalf, or to articulate a way of effective mobilization to combat some historic and long-standing injustice - by any means necessary. We are never told who to fight or how to "fight the power"; and Black militancy is rarely depicted. I believe we are not fully in control of our story, because it is not written for us.

We must ask, who is paying these people? Who is funding their documentaries? What institution is funding the research, and who is footing the bill for some academic to spend years digging through archives, and crisscrossing the country or globe for tidbits of information? When these questions are answered we will understand who pulls the purse strings, and who stands in the shadows looking over the shoulders of the  men and women tasked with bringing our story to the light of day. The scariest part of the matter is that Blacks do not see their own behavior as being driven by media, status, or other external forces;   they believe what they perceive of Black culture are actually authentic expressions of the people's souls. They believe they are in the real world when they are actually asleep and living in an artificial matrix.

Why is this important? Authors, artist and other personalities are under tremendous pressure to conform to society's demands or bend to the will of whatever person or institution is paying them. Therefore it stands to reason the creators of various forms of media content with our narrative in mind will consciously or subconsciously sanitize, obscure, or otherwise whitewash and suppress their real conclusions.

Maybe the author does not want to paint a picture that is too bleak for intellectuals to reflect on and replace a detailed analysis of the subject with the over use of euphemisms. While others may not want to offer their most scathing critique of the facts they are analyzing, fearing the perception they are being  too hard on Black people.

Yet others may paint a picture that is worst than the actual circumstances that existed, so as not to deviate from their benefactor's gloomy expectations; or they pathologically pursue objectivity and miss the mark of truth, because they want to be balanced. Can a Black or white author really be radical while contracted to one of the very few major publishing houses left? Harriet Washington author of: *Medical Apartheid*, a ground breaking book on the American medical establishment's dark history of research on African American bodies revealed the following:

*In fact some otherwise well-meaning people wish to censor analysis of troubled research with African Americans, as I discovered firsthand, to my surprise. I was elated when a professor at a U.S. medical school summoned me to her office, explaining that she wanted to hear all about the book I was writing....I eagerly began to describe my work, only to be cut off before I completed the first sentence. Bolting upright in her chair, she vehemently informed me that the topic of the book was taboo. "It's a terrible thing that you are doing. You are going to make African Americans afraid of medical research and physicians! You cannot write this book!" As she glared at me, her face became contorted with anger, suffused with blood, and her breathing grew rapid. For a moment, I was stunned into silence, because nothing had prepared me for her reaction... I was also a bit surprised that a white academic whose discussions and syllabus had evinced no interest or expertise in the matter should lecture me, an experienced African American medical writer, about health communication with African Americans. 11*

Harriet Washington's experience is not unique. It was reported in The New York Times: That Historian Julius S. Scott's dissertation on the Haitian Revolt was -rejected by mainstream publishers for three decades. "Dr. Scott's manuscript was originally rejected by Indiana University Press. He then signed a contract with Oxford University press but dropped the project because he disagreed with revisions suggest by fellow academics who had reviewed his draft at the request of Oxford's editors."(12) Professor Nicole Hannah-Jones received national backlash from (mostly) Right-wing academics after she published her "1619 Project" which is her study of American history as it pertains to the African and European contact and relationships beginning with the first slaves sold by Dutch traders to Virginia's English colonist in 1619.

Such pressure is not limited to Black authors one (white male) author whose name is now lost to me was commissioned to write a book about the ethnic cleansing of African Americans in North Carolina's Forsythe county, in the early 20th century. The author recounted how he researched the subject and found out there were not just one ethnically cleansed town but many of them throughout the south - which he used the census data to find out; and how he was told to shelve the book after it was written. How many others are faced with such dilemmas? After I finished my first book *Reflections of the Son*, a Black male asked me: "*What, you wrote a book about the hood so white people can understand?*" I asked him *'why would he ask me some dumb shit like that?'* He replied: "*Because they the only ones who read books*?" This male was not the brightest, but he was on to something. He was tapped into the unspoken question that all authors and artist must grapple with. Who am I making this for? What is my purpose for creating this? Do I want money or to authentically create/ tell my story, no matter the outcome? The question was an easy one for me. I know who my audience was and what I wanted to say to them; and I knew I would not be compromised.

If a person is writing in order to make The New York Times best seller list, receive a Pulitzer award, make Oparah's book club list, to receive tenured professorship, or for mainstream recognition their work will not carry the same force or energy that it would if it were a manifesto to their people. Imagine the Biblical story of the Exodus was written by Jewish scribes for the Egyptian aristocracy as an academic curriculum on the Hebrew experience in bondage, then imagine the scribes had been sponsored by Egypt's administrative priestocracy, the Exodus would have never become the Jewish spiritual origin story that it has been for thousands of years. There is a perfect example of just this very scenario.

Despite Flavius Josephus (born AD. 37 – died 90 ?) being a well educated elite Jew versed in all the sectarian ecclesiastical law and history of his people, his book *Jewish Antiquities* has never reached the level of a sacred text by the Jewish people. *Jewish Antiquities* as a historical document is only surpassed by *the Old Testament* in providing information about the ancient Jewish people, religion, wars, prophets, persecutions, and culture. The problem with Josephus is that when he wrote *Jewish Antiquities* he was a Roman citizen and considered a traitor to the Jewish people, because he surrendered to the Romans after the failed Jewish revolt in 66-73 Ad. *Jewish Antiquities* was written in Greek in a Greco-Roman style of narration, and  important figures in Jewish history were treated like they were sages and philosophers in the Greek tradition. As a historic literary text of the ancient world *Jewish Antiquities* is surpassed by none, but because Josephus was receiving Roman patronage his writings never entered the Jewish  spiritual tradition as part of their literary legacy.

Returning to the subject at hand, if  books, movies, and documentary films chronicling the Black experience are not for us then who are they for, and what is the agenda? Considering the marketing venues, political posture, clinical tone, and content of the books and other forms of media,  this  material is written and produced for academic consumers. I believe the true goal of this literature is to educate the next generation of  intellectuals (Black and white) and college students, who will work in corporate industry, philanthropy, government administration, and policy planning. I believe these books and other forms of media are created to soften a new generation of leadership to the sufferings of Black people. The target audience being white middle class, who must be taught about the 'sins of their fathers'; so they can help repair the damage that has been done in their name. These books and other media are not produced to raise the consciousness of Blacks, but to raise the consciousness of whites; as such, the content is tailored to their unique psychology and intellectual spectrum. Whatever the case, making them sympathetic to Black disadvantages and viewing our situation with compassion seems to be the aim of Black academics, who get mainstream recognition.

It is clear this content is not being produced in order for Blacks to develop community strategies to help them to confront a hostile empire. The people making this material are professional lecturers, directors, sociologists, professors, historians, journalists, and fellows connected to think tanks or universities. They make their living in the world of academia speaking to the highly educated. Usually in lecture halls full of whites and Asians. Most have never been on the ground organizing the people they are talking about. And any contact with common people is based on research.

It makes no difference that these books with their findings are not for us. The information presented in these forums finds its way down to the masses through their own consumption of books, literature, articles, and film. The major themes, talking points, and conclusions end up in the mouths of misguided auto-didactics, who quote and cite these people as legitimate and competent authorities. The problem with this picture is that compromised information (sanitized, distorted, manipulated, or exaggerated) tailored for progressive (or conservative) consumers is influencing the opinions of well-meaning people.

Local leadership cite these books and films as if they are the latest most cutting edge analysis and commentary on the subject. The power of these various forms of media in shaping the Black imagination and self-perception is impressive and cannot be overlooked. We are unwittingly marching to the drum of progressive and liberal literature, opinion, and world view. However, after reading about or watching their historic suffering Blacks are left without a plan of action. Blacks seek out this material thinking it was written to empower them, but it does not have that effect, and they are left simultaneously both more informed of facts and more clueless without direction.

## DOES THE POLITICAL LEFT HELP PERPETUATE OUR VICTIM STATUS?

Although there exists a growing number of Black writers who self-identify as conservative I think it can be said with confidence that the majority of Black intellectuals are largely under the sway of the political left. It is the left that is the most welcoming to Black intellectuals and who provides them a platform, coverage, and positive exposure. However, this warm embrace and exposure comes at the price of strict leftist orthodoxy. Meaning, Black intellectuals must conform to the leftist social critique and agenda (worldview, logic, language, and plan). The leftist agenda is a broad one concerned with global reforms (or revolution). At the top of the list are an overhaul of capitalism, social justice for women, minorities, gay rights, and environmental protection policy. The leftist agenda does not necessarily align (nor conflict) with the priorities of Black liberation politics, which is in a stage of under-development by comparison. The Left's agenda concerns itself with the following questions:

How do they (progressives & liberals) run the system where they have come into power  (gained democratic majority) on the local, state, national, and international levels?

To achieve women's equality or superiority in all areas of society.

How to provide fairness/ justice for as many as possible?

Do they have to destroy the current economic (capitalist) system in order to accomplish their vision?

How much national/social conflict (civil war) would the total imposition of their vision bring about?

Do they make a coalition with like minded racial minorities at the expense of backward/ conservative whites?

Or is it easier to achieve their goals without disturbing white racial harmony?

Can this agenda be implemented while a large percentage (majority) of white males are alienated? Etcetera.

This agenda is supported by an entire infrastructure of well-funded influential political leaders, youth, business leaders, universities, academics, intellectuals, think tanks, charities, NGOs, religious organizations, philanthropic organizations, and advocacy groups. Who are only matched in funding, organization, passion, Machiavellianism, and ridiculousness by the Right-wing Conservative political machinery.

Nevertheless, the agenda of these mostly educated elites are not the first concerns of Black liberation politics, whose first questions of concern centers around:

How do we organize our families, wealth, and institutions so that they produce healthy men and women able resist the slings and arrows of the empire?

How do we accumulate enough wealth and power that will insulate us from historic minority vulnerabilities?

Is it possible to penetrate and manipulate the political system so that it works for us?

Can we organize the necessary political machinery from the current stock of stubborn, pessimistic, downtrodden Black folk?

How do Black people function as a state without distinct physical territory?

How prepared will we be if there is a show down between us and elements of the empire and what will that look like?

How do we stop the addiction, blood-letting and fratricide taking place in our urban centers that is wasting so much of our human and intellectual potential?

How do we slow down and reverse the mass incarceration of our males and females while seeing to it that they are punished for their crimes, violent or otherwise?

How do we overthrow the white supremacist order while fighting on so many fronts. Do we have allies and who are they?

Do we trust these (conservative) people who say they are color blind and just want fairness or  the (liberal) people who say they see our plight and that our struggles  are the same?

Can we trust anybody?

These are the major concerns for me and those I follow philosophically, intellectually, and spiritually. LGBT rights, climate change, open arms immigration policy, and gun reform are not my top priorities. I am even opposed to the last two on principal. I believe many politically minded Blacks feel the same way, but they are not given the platforms for their opinions. And others  are afraid to say otherwise because it may offend powerful forces (benefactors) who provide help, but do not accept difference of opinion.

Liberals not only give us platforms but have even resorted to lecturing Blacks about our own oppression. A Black male was telling me about a class he was taking where the curriculum consisted of how the 'Black male was traumatized and is suffering from PTSD and high levels of stress' blah blah blah. I was not surprised to hear that a white man was overseeing this class. I warned him that he could not build himself up with the guilt of white  people and that in my opinion  liberals could be just as dangerous as the right-wing nuts.

Later I met the teacher in question and true to form his discussions often deviated to the victimization of Blacks and women. He was certainly a socialist and feminist, but none of that bothered me.  What bothered me was the constant mention of Blacks as victims, and how the other Black males in the room relished in his simplistic paradigm of evil-white-male capitalist versus the helpless everybody else. The Black males in the class were in awe of someone with academic training who  treated them like real students. Some behaved like lackeys and took offense on his behalf whenever I challenged his  interpretation of sociological data.  I also noticed that he was not as well informed on facts and history of topics outside his sociological field. This lead me to believe that he would be unable to form a complete picture of the true human condition.

Privately I warned him that Blacks were bombarded with stories of lynching, slavery, rape, murder, throughout their entire lives - and it was having an adverse effect of their mental health. He accepted the critique and conveyed to me that he had 'never thought of that.' He was not a bad person, in fact, we engaged in a broad range of intellectual discourse. My major problem with the left is their intolerance of dissent.

They readily accept the idea that Blacks have been disadvantaged because of racist policies and laws. However to be part of their orbit you must accept that capitalism is evil, and individualism (in all forms) is evil. Individualism to them only means: selfish, egoistic, and greedy. They really do want to empower the state and use it to impose a collective will on others; and for some bizarre reason they assume the people in charge will always be enlightened and good. That said, many Blacks are comfortable with their seat at the leftist table and gladly forfeit intellectual independence. I have chosen to listen to my ancestors who warned us of half-baked theories and people pushing utopian ideas of human nature. In other books I have leveled scathing critiques of Right-wingers and so I feel no need to be fair and balanced at this moment.

# THE SIX PILLARS OF HEALTHY HISTORY

History is not news and must not be confused as such. We cannot confuse the objective documentation of present tense local, national, or international facts with the duty of telling of our grand narrative. The objective documentation of facts must be done in all sincerity and honesty so that those vested in truth may make sound decisions in their daily lives as it pertains to running their households, businesses, and social institutions. The professionals tasked with the objective documentation of present tense facts are called journalists.

Journalists are not historians, historians have another goal as it pertains to recording and preserving facts. When it comes to the preserving and conveying our truth neither the journalist nor historian are qualified to transmit what will become the internalized spiritual saga of a community or nation. Transmitting our spiritual saga to the next generation must serve some basic communal functions. What are we trying to accomplish with the narration of our past? What is it we want our children to know and believe? If the purpose is to recount some facts without consideration of the power and force of the human narrative then we have been seduced by the Western lie of 'objectivity.' We who contemplate the destiny of nations know with certainty that if our history does not fulfill the following needs then it is not worth telling:

_Inspire them to aim for some concept of summum bonum;

_Provide optimism and context to their current reality;

_Celebrate their great ones;

_Teach them cautionary tales, warning them not to befall the errors of their ancestors;

_Convey to them that their actions are the focus  of the story and the determining factor in  their/world survival;

_Give them an enemy (physical or idea) for whom every ill  in the world has emanated from.

These are the pillars of a healthy historical narrative. People tell their history the way they do because there is a healing in it. This also is why history, song, and poetry are  synonymous in the ancient world; the Greeks had their Iliad, Jews have the Torah, Muslims the Qur'an, hadeeth, and Sirah, Hindus their Vedas, and Africans their Griots. In all traditions history, philosophy, religion, and law are transmitted by the same  medium of rhythmic hymn. These are/were mature people and civilizations - objectivity was not their goal. What they had in mind was first the formation of a group identity, then the celebration of this group/national identity. This had to be achieved before there could be a unity of purpose, tribute to great people, warnings, and commandments to obey the laws.

There is healing and lessons in the Jewish story of the "Exodus;" there is healing and lessons in the Sirah of the prophet Muhammad and the early Islamic community; there is healing and guidance in the history of the American revolution. These 'histories' were crafted not simply to document facts but to inspire and teach people. Our children should receive their historical instruction as if it was religious instruction either at home, or in a setting conducive to transmitting sensitive spiritual  knowledge from griot to mature vessels.

In any case, by a person who is not simply trying to get children to recall social studies facts for a passing grade, but who has in mind that these narratives are the foundation to the future generation's conscious and subconscious motivations and guiding principles. Those who insist on teaching young children about slavery, lynching, and oppression before their minds can actually grasp complex political concepts are out of their minds. They know nothing about development of people. I find that those plagued by victim-narratives develop them very young. If their internal narrative is not the product of school or the media it is the poison of the parents and family indoctrination. I found a girl of six who was already of the opinion that her silky hair was better than the kinky type, but her darker skin was worst than light skin.

I pose is this question: What is the value of learning your history if it serves only the goal and purpose of constantly affirming or reliving your victimization and suffering? What is the purpose of history and information devoid of strategic context? What is the value of raw data in the form of statistics and facts enumerated in chronological order? Are we telling our story or cataloging our misery by century, decade, year, month, and day? Is the goal to inform without inflaming? To ponder without zeal or thirst for revenge? To intellectualize the suffering of our people on slave ships? To speculate on the stress levels of Jim Crow negroes? To pity them and us? To justify our failings and slow progress? To explain our litany of bizarre behaviors?

The unintended consequence of history without context is that many subconsciously absorb the most common theme  and that common denominator is victimhood. This feeds a cult of victimhood that dominates the Black psyche like few other themes. A people's history that does not inspire them is not history but the slow  drip of trauma given in small enough doses  not to cause a heart attack. This debate over Black history is not limited to  books, and documentaries but to  actual  physical  institutions. While  writing  this  section I stumbled  upon  an  article  that  captures   the  issues   raised  in  this argument. In the Smithsonian magazine issue entitled:  "Black  in America"/September 2016, an issue that commemorates the opening of the National Museum of African American History and Culture, I found the following quote:

*One of the biggest challenges we faced was wrestling with the widely differing assumptions of what the museum should be. There were those who felt that it was impossible, in a federally supported museum, to explore candidly some of the painful aspects of history, such as  slavery and discrimination. Others felt strongly that the new museum had the responsibility to shape the mindset of future generations, and should do so without discussing moments that might depict African Americans simply as victims - in essence, create a museum that emphasized famous firsts and positive images. Conversely, some believed  that this institution should be a holocaust museum that depicted "what they did to us."....I hope that the museum can play a small part in helping our nation grapple with its tortured racial past. And maybe even help us find a bit of reconciliation. 13*

By Lonnie G. Bunch

All of the issues raised in this essay can be found in the above quote: First there is the "differing assumptions" among Blacks as to what Black history should mean; Second there is the problem of benefactors and what the influence of outside money does to influence the telling  (or not telling)  of the Black experience; Third those who thought the purpose of the museum was to "shape the mindset of future generations" and present positive images for Blacks to avoid the victim-narrative; Fourth those who think the telling of Black history means telling: "what they did to us."Fifth the fact that the museum is for "the nation to grapple with its tortured past and maybe even help us [who is us?] find a bit of reconciliation." Not necessarily an edifice built for Black people so they may celebrate, ponder and present to the world their American legacy. I wonder if similarly situated museums wrestle with their mission statement.

# FAILURE OF LEADERSHIP TO USE THE POSITIVE BLACK NARRATIVE TO BUILD MOVEMENT

In the end, Black "leadership" on the community level, in academia, industry, or national figures with a presence in mainstream culture fail to utilize the power of the Black historical narrative as a tool to mobilize the young and old around a set of principles, or weapon to defend us against our detractors. The result is that history remains a yoke and shackle, that burdens and shames Black people instead of inspiring them.

A growing segment of educated Blacks and so-called Black "leadership" made up of politicians, clergy, intellectuals, and heads of organizations feel that it is their duty to prove the "humanity" of Black people to every person who doubts it. When disaster strikes and the Black body politic is angered, enraged or saddened by a new senseless killing they do not channel Black anger and sadness into something productive like local or national self-help organization; that will precipitate a new consciousness, awareness, solidarity, and resolve to resist.

Their concern is to put out Black fire, moderate tensions, cool hostilities so nothing (no one) radical emerges from the chaos. Their goal is to get Black youth to talk it out and getting white people to see race from the Black perspective. Ultimately they are trying to convince white people to empathize. But there is something wrong when your primary strategy revolves around town hall meetings and telling people how sad you feel; and there is something particularly spineless when your only  plan of action  centers  around trying to convince others of your humanity.

When a Black person is abused or shot by some agency or civilian the first thing that occurs from our "leadership" is a shallow critique of historic 'community relations,' vis a vis Black and white or Blacks and law enforcement. The second thing is to dodge any discussion of  'Black crime rates' hurled at them by adept propagandists. The third is to explain how we are supposed to engage law enforcement if confronted and have "the talk" with our boys; which is basically a plan action for displaying exaggerated meekness in the face of irrational authority.

No wonder the youth go out  and burn 'their own communities' when there is civil unrest. Nobody has a plan of action to mobilize them to do anything else - wanton destruction is their default option. They burn that which is familiar because nobody has instructed them on what (if anything) is worthy of destruction and what is not. All these talkers are of the same ilk. They all use the same language: Black bodies, our humanity, micro aggressions, white supremacy, carceral state, systemic racism. They are so predictable. Their speech is measured but their arguments lack the force  and refinement required to confront professional sophistry. The visible Black "leadership" are animals of defense, they are always cornered, always unraveling the confusing misinformation of our enemies. They are always explaining and correcting the record and trying to be professional and in the middle of the road. Black leaders are allergic to radical concepts; however, where there is no radical thought  no radical action cannot occur. We have no leaders in the mainstream.

# SECTION III

# HOW POSITIVE NARRATIVE WAS LOST, ABANDONED, AND REJECTED

The cult of victimhood, though not new, has recently come to dominate the psychology of many males and females, but this did not happen over night. It was a process or many processes working simultaneously over decades in different places. In 1988 I was ten and can remember African and Black nationalist symbols were a part of mainstream Black culture. Wearing clothing apparel or medallions with Afrocentric themes (the Black fist was my favorite) meant one was conscious and unapologetically Black. It was in the dress, hair styles, cultural art, the language and the music. Groups like 'Earth Wind and Fire' had been depicting Egyptian symbols on their albums since the 70s. In the 1980s and early 90s Rap music was flourishing in New York and nationwide, to embrace one's Blackness was to be cool. Malcolm X was a clear icon to be emulated. As a teenager in the early 90s my vague understanding of Black existence was that we were against "the system" whatever that was. This was a commonly held belief among many of my peers.

During this same period the music, literature, art and politics reflected a clear message of Black pride and militancy. There was even a healthy strain of self-criticism within the culture. Rap music was notorious for castigating gangbanging, weed smokers, and people who rob, stole, and kill others for a living. Rap artist did not celebrate criminality and no one claimed to be a criminal; so called gangster rap was in its infancy and only a marginal segment of the culture. Criminals were usually the target of scathing rap lyrics, but this mindset did not last. *"Criminal Minded"* went from being a Hip Hop political critique of the system and urban America by KRS One, to a personal philosophy of Tupac, under the name of "T.H.U.G. L.I.F.E."

Within fifteen years - not even ten years after the Million Man March by the mid 2000s -  I noticed a shift in thought. Discussions about "Black" issues were ridiculed by a large body of the Black males I encountered. Talking about "Black politics" was unfashionable, it simply was not cool and considered irrelevant. In prison there was a small circle of us then in our twenties, thirties and forties (born in sixties and seventies)  who got funny looks and jokes for talking about the "Black man" and being "revolutionaries." There was always a caricaturizing  of our actual discussions which ranged in subject, from law and philosophy to science and history. Other males would challenge us about "blaming the white man for everything," which was their impression/stereotype  of our gatherings.  They did not know what we were talking about,  but assumed that we were living out the common trope of the Black militant that is the butt of many jokes in Black comedic cinema. They were fed up with the discussions of "the  white man" and felt that such talk was no longer legitimate. Black people were "post racial" before it became a hip political concept.

I got a sense from older males that they felt betrayed by Black nationalist rhetoric, as if it had been fruitless in their eyes. As for younger males I got the impression they were willfully ignorant of the subject matter of Black liberation, and secondly, afraid of the seriousness of being a responsible man. It was clear to me they were afraid of State violence against any person or group who advocated "Black Power." This was expressed to me in many forms from jokes to wide-eyed warnings. The fear of State repression is very much present in the consciousness of Black males. The Black Panthers are a potent symbol for many males I talk to, they are held in high regard for their militant stance, actions, and charitable giving ; but I cannot help but think that the Panthers' ultimate defeat also looms in the imagination. Most of the males I talk to have no clue what the Panthers actually stood for politically, because most don't understand differences between Marxism, socialism, capitalism, or revolution; it is only the Panther's infamy and militant message that holds the attention of males.

In general, the young were not serious about anything except drug abuse, gang life, and religious hypocrisy. Apart from sports and pop culture they possess little factual knowledge only fragmented ideas and concepts held together by ignorance. My peers thought it was safer and profitable to be gangbangers rather than "revolutionaries" and became the vanguard of a gang wave. The consequences for embracing of Red, Black, and Green flag made them paranoid, so they settled for just red and blue flags. During this period politically conscious literature disappeared from prisoner's personal libraries, to be replaced by "hood book" or "urban lit." Overnight books that were required reading by young prisoners were abandoned. Works like: *The Soledad Brothers, Blood in My Eye, The Isis Papers, Soul on Ice, Destruction of a Black Civilization, author J.A. Rogers books, Anthony Browder's books, (The Browder files), and Na'im Akbar's* portfolio became rare, and then forgotten.

Books with well placed critiques of the global system of power were never picked up or heard of, by a new generation. I asked the older generation of males 'what they thought was responsible for this total loss of (radical & racial) consciousness?' The first thing they point to is the prison administration's crackdown on militant Black males, by placing influential leaders in isolation units for decades at a time, and punishing others with a thousand cuts; making Black nationalism a difficult philosophy to practice. On the other hand, I was informed by men I consider honest - who were witness to this period of prison - that too many Black radicals equated political militancy with violence, and did not use their organization effectively. Suggesting they were themselves , in part, responsible for the violent crackdown on "militant" groups.  The second factor they point to is religion.

# A DEFINITION OF CONSCIOUSNESS

I must first articulate what I mean when I use the terms political consciousness or Black consciousness. Having consciousness means I, as an individual (or group), believe and acknowledge there are people in the world who are actively seeking to keep me subservient, and want to use my body and energy to enrich themselves. And if I allow them they will drain me of all of my power and reduce me to a slave. Consciousness is a self-aware commitment to resist all deceptions and manipulators, by any means necessary. The conscious person's second order of business is to not allow themselves to be used to hurt or disadvantage others - especially poor, uneducated, or Blacks. The conscious person is not a racist, he is fully aware of how race is used to divide and conquer others. Consciousness means you have a very deep connection to all of humanity.

As a conscious person everything that I do becomes an act of resistance. Everything I do and think is potentially criminal because it is subversive. All of my actions personal, public, or private have the intent on undermining the State, and those who want to keep me subjugated. The terms consciousness and revolutionary are very close, however, there is a difference. The revolutionary is planning to or is engaged in violent acts to overthrow the present political order. Whereas the conscious person is engaged in day-to-day activity to loosen the grip of the negative powers that control their lives.

When the conscious person steals from the State it is not thievery, it is appropriation. It is doing what is right and righteous. Waste is a serious crime to the conscious person, it is just as offensive as murder. How can there be waste while so many are in need? He who steals is better than those who allow something to be thrown away, while others are hungry and in need. However, stealing from the people is the very high crime. Conscious people are givers and takers. They give to the people and take from the (unjust) State. The conscious person does not want trouble, but exist in a state of total psychological rebellion to the establishment. The conscious person will never allow themselves to be humiliated by an agent of the State. He or she is prepared (mentally/ physically) for violent confrontation in order to preserve his dignity, and to be an example for others of what it means to be a man/ or woman.

The conscious person believes that if the government does not exist  to protect and serve the people it has no legitimacy. Therefore any hostile action against the State to prevent oppression is morally justified. The conscious person cannot cooperate if she feels that common people are being sold out. The conscious person sees the actions of the majority as being guided by instinct and conditioning. The common people are not acting for the good of themselves. They are acting from their conditioning, training, or out of fear. The actions of the common person are not political, or for 'the greater good,' they are not symbolic, they are individualistic. The common people are domesticated.

The conscious person does not smile out of fear. He does not show his teeth in order to make others feel comfortable. The conscious person does not want his oppressors comfortable. The conscious person does not smile or laugh except when around true people. The smile or laugh  that is not around true people is only a mask. The conscious person does not scream if he is in pain. He must suffer in silence until death comes. The conscious person must be articulate,  he must be able to convey his inner reality to others in order to raise their level of consciousness.

The conscious person must be well read and articulate because he must stand up for himself and others by using his words. They must be articulate because after all the words end there is only violence left. The conscious person understands he/she cannot back down or all is lost. The conscious person cannot be fat or out of shape because they must always be in control of their body and mind. The conscious person must tame his fears, at no time can he  lose control. Control over the senses is at the core of being conscious. The conscious person does not hoard food and exploit people for profit. He does fair trade and fair business. To manipulate others is a humiliation of himself, it only proves he is small inside and afraid of poverty and hunger.

Conscious people revere the spirit of Malcolm X. He is an example of the highest manifestation of righteous consciousness. Being 'woke' and Consciousness are not the same, consciousness requires sacrifice of money, status, power, or life for higher principles. Consciousness is achieved by learning correct conduct from others. You either have  to be raised by conscious parents or instructed by righteous men and women. If you have not consumed conscious or revolutionary literature and then made the necessary emotional and psychological adjustments to your behavior and thinking then you are not conscious. If you are not ready at any moment to  engage your oppressor then you are not conscious. Being conscious is not normal state of being, it is a mental state of elevated thinking and self-awareness where the thinker knows that s/he is actively engaged in resisting the conditioning of  State propaganda, corporate marketing, and the entertainment media machine.

Being conscious is the act of resisting all the forces who are trying to manipulate you for their own agenda; whether it is to use you for a soldier of war, political pawn, or brainless consumer. Consciousness is the act of preventing these entities from brainwashing you, or being indoctrinating with a false sense of self. Consciousness is waking up everyday knowing you may have to suffer for your principles or for others, nonetheless, embracing life without fear. You can be conscious and still subscribe to many different belief systems. You can be: Atheist, Muslim Christian, Buddhist,  socialist, or believe in capitalism.

************

# NOTE:

This section of this essay is not a definitive history of Islam in America, it is based entirely on my experience of Islam in Camden New Jersey and particularly the New Jersey prison system. I took my Shahada in 1997 as a free man and entered the New Jersey prison system in 1999. It is now 2022 and I have seen the religious community change over that period of time, and have documented the trends as I recall them. This essay is based on first-hand observation, conversations, research, and consultation. I have painstakingly presented my ideas to others for their analysis, opinion and critique. Not surprisingly others have confirmed that my feelings, experiences, and observations were not mine alone, but widely shared thoughts. In addition others have pointed out things that I had not noticed and added their own commentary. Remember this essay is about the attitude change in Black men as it relates to other men, his community, and his world view.

## RELIGION AND LOSS OF CONSCIOUSNESS

Religion is the refuge for those who want positive change in their lives, but have no idea of what that looks like. Instead they trust others (who appear to be righteous) to guide them by a set of beliefs and principles that have withstood the test of time. Men will always find a religion to help guide them when they are feeling empty, stumbling in darkness, and or craving something more than material satisfaction. The benefits of religion on the lives of some men behind bars in undeniable. Islam and Christianity have taught men discipline, how to read, write, and think of something other than their next high. Malcolm X is a perfect example of the power of faith. However, if religion wants to take credit for bringing out the best in man, in terms of his intellectual and moral refinement, then it must also accept blame for bringing the worst out of him and assume responsibility for his intellectual deterioration and turning some into complete fools. I have learned we must not allow our religion to be high jacked by those whose only prerogative is the pursuit of power and not moral order on earth and the spiritual refinement of humanity.

********

Through speaking to others and reading radical literature I heard about a tradition of political intellectualism and militancy that existed in prison, but when I arrived I could only find a trace of it. There were still small groups of men who walked the talk and circulated conscious literature. Some were certified radicals who had been in the Black Panthers, BLA or other associations and incarcerated behind their beliefs and actions. There were many who had changed their 'slave names' to African or Islamic attributes. They would try and help incoming young men find their way by conversation and the circulation of 'revolutionary' ideas.

The books that were handed to young men ranged from novels, history (African mostly), sociology, psychology, science, Egyptology, and anthropology. The writers were European, African, Black American, Asian, South American, and Russian. The study of law was almost mandated for every young male entering the system. Older men were always engaged in academic discussions about precedent or recent case law, or Supreme Court decisions and how to interpret these laws and apply them in novel ways to individual cases. The goal was to spark the young male's interest in knowledge and generally lead him to the road of self reflection, enlightenment, and behavioral refinement.

Nevertheless, by the early 2000s when I entered New Jersey's maximum security prison system in my early twenties the

105

revolutionary spirit was dim. There was still plenty of revolutionary and enlightening literature in circulation, but the audience that was receptive to these books was shrinking. The prison system that I had heard about where men were militant and striving for political awareness was just a shell of itself. I mostly encountered inmates of a very low caliber on the organizational, intellectual, and maturity spectrum. More often than not I encounter drug addicted males, and males whose only stimulation was  sectarian based religious literature, which was soon followed by a wave of gang culture.

In the early 2000s inmates began reading "hood books" like they were going out of style. Morbid tales of the drug game, robbery, pimping, prostitutes, femme  fatales,  double crossing, and killing became the preferred leisure for the young reader who wanted to distract themselves from prison life. These books were everywhere and being talked about by everyone. Many women were also attracted to this "literature", which purports to vividly portray the dark side of human nature.  In reality many of these books are poorly written, not to mention feeble attempts to describe the underworld by those who barely scratched the surface of that life.

The older prisoners (40-60) I spoke to were  witness to three decades of prison evolution. When I asked them 'how Black consciousness among the population had disappeared?' many blamed it on  religion. They particularly claimed that Islam had absorbed within its ranks militant minded males, and took Muslims into a radical (fundamentalist) direction. They believed that Sunni Islam (as practiced in prison) had pacified the Black males within the prison system and turned them away from the political and revolutionary teachings they needed to understand their situation and solve their problems.  I listened to such opinions and contemplated their validity, but it was only with years of observation did I come to the conclusion that statements such as this were not without some merit.

Since the 1950s Muslims have continuously been the most powerful force in prison for Black men.  In their opinion, Islam  now focused black male creative energy primarily towards spirituality and the afterlife. There was no worry of Christianity because it was never popular among  a certain segment of the urban males in the New Jersey, New York, Philadelphia tri-state area, it was always seen as "the white man's religion" and associated with weakness, passivity, and hypocrisy. Black males know that Christians were good people because most of our families were Christian, but that was the problem - they were too damn good. Christianity was viewed as having no place for militant or intellectual males. The perception is that it induces cognitive sleep, produces con men, and advocates meekness. It was something for old people and women.

Political consciousness bases its entire philosophy on building the next generation of thinkers, resisting the State, and the willingness to use violence - as a last resort- if need be. This is a rejection of the Christian tradition of humility and submission to a White god, and vow to 'study war no more.' The false representation of Martin Luther King both during his life and after his death has cost the Black church  millions of souls. Historically, only the most militant preachers have been accepted as revolutionaries. During the late 1980s and 90s, prisons were cracking down on Black nationalist and militant organizations - which had been spreading through the nation's prison system since the 1950s, 60s & 70s.

Among the most popular of these  groups are the Black Panthers, Black Liberation Army (BLA), Nation of Islam & the 5%  Nation of Gods and Earths (on offshoot of the Nation of Islam). The Nation of Islam had a physical presence in urban areas for decades in the form of temples of worship, business establishments and social organizations. The 5% Nation of Gods & Earths was thoroughly embedded in New York city subculture and  as a result was spread nationwide through Hip hop culture.

There were also many smaller organizations with no national recognition, some of which were political some quasi-religious. The influence of prisons on the Black criminal subculture is undeniable and likewise the influence of the Black male on the larger national culture is irrefutable. State and Federal 'correctional facilities' are the meeting places of males from different regions, and as a result  knowledge is exchanged, connections are made, and values are shared. In prison Black males interact with and learn from people from diverse classes and ethnicities. Prisons take on the qualities of criminal universities where observation, graft, posturing, predatory psychology and hustling are part of the curriculum. However, other things are also learned like religion, philosophy, morals, cooperation, and etiquette; everything that is learned returns back to urban centers and enters the fabric of the broader culture through music, migration or custom.

During this same period (1975-1990s) Islam in the Black community was undergoing many transformations. The militant Black nationalist brand of Islam of the NOI was losing ground to "orthodox" Sunni Islam which is a multi-ethnic religion and dismisses nationalism as incompatible with the religion's doctrine. Wallace. D. Mohammad  (Warithudeen) son of Elijah Muhammad spiritual leader and founder of the Nation of Islam is credited with the first stage of the organization's transformation to Sunni Islam, when he assumed leadership of the Nation Of Islam after his father's death in 1975 and took those who followed him in a new direction.

The first indicator of the paradigm shift in religious thought was evinced in the organization's new name: WORLD COMMUNITY OF AL-ISLAM IN THE WEST. One of my mentors (who was from Philadelphia) claimed responsibility for introducing Sunni Islam into the New Jersey prison system. He informed me that when he arrived in  the New Jersey prison system in the early 1980s there were no Sunni communities established. This is a highly respected man who elders nationwide looked up to, I do not know him to be a liar nor can I imagine him fabricating something like that. For the record, there were already  Sunni Muslims in America, but they were not effective in converting Black Americans.

According to Wallace D. Mohammad: *"During the [1960s] a different breed  came [into  the Nation of Islam]....With the revolt of Blacks, the civil revolt, the Temple of Islam offered a strong appeal for those militant blacks; so some of them from the Black panthers and others began to come into the community. I don't think all of them were religious members of those organizations, but they were people who had been influenced by those organizations. They began to join the community in the sixties, and I believe it was the emphasis on business, business development, business growth along with black pride that attracted those people to the community," 14*

The transition from Nation of Islam to Sunni Islam was not a clean break from one stage to the next, but more like a slow metamorphosis that took decades to reach its current manifestation, which has many incarnations of Sunni Islam. This change occurred in small pockets in different cities and prisons. The years the Nation Of Islam was run by Elijah Muhammad up until his death is called the "First Resurrection" which signifies the lifting of Black men and Women out of their dumb, deaf, and blind state of being which white supremacy had reduced them to; the actual name of the organization was "*The Lost Found Nation Of Islam.*"

The second stage of this transformation is referred to as the "Second Resurrection" which constitutes the time period that Wallace D. Mohammad moved Black Muslims into the global Sunni Muslim community. Writer Sherman A. Jackson now classifies the period we are now in as the "Third Resurrection" which is supposed to be the era when Black people assume mastery over Sunni Islamic scholarship in all the crucial areas of Qur'anic and Hadeeth science, interpretation, and authentication; which are the foundations to Islamic law making or jurisprudence (usul–al fiqh). The essence of "Third Resurrection" is to make the Black community a self-reliant authority in their own religious affairs, so we don't have to be the unknowing subjects (dupes) of a foreign-born ecclesiastical (Middle-Eastern & Asian) caste.15

Wallace D. Mohammad's particular brand of Sunni Islam gained a foothold in the prison system for a while but soon lost ground to more so called 'orthodox traditions.' The most rigid of them is the "Salafist" minhaj (way or path) - a popular movement within the global Islamic community that currently exerts a great influence on what is considered authentic tradition. Salafist erroneously believe they can make takfir and determine who is or is not Muslim. According to the Salafist strain of Islam both Wallace D. Mohammad and  Elijah Muhammad are viewed as heretics and are not even Muslim; Wallace. D. Mohammad because (inter alia) he states that everything in the Qur'an is not literal, but only allegorical and Elijah Muhammad because he claimed that W. D. Fard was god incarnate and he himself was the  messenger of god - a title reserved for the prophet Muhammad Ibn Abdullah (SAW) of Arabia. Thirty or forty years ago to make a statement that these men were not Muslims could have spelled a death sentence. Now it is considered an  obvious fact of Salafist creed.

Salafist, many of whom were once themselves members of the WORLD COMMUNITY OF AL ISLAM, now consider Wallace D. Mohammad and his followers "Warithuhdeen Muslims" good intentioned but religiously misguided people who fail to follow strict Islamic law of the Qur'an &  Sunna (traditions) of Muhammad. It is believed that some of their Islamic practices are not rooted in Islam but religious innovations or bid'ah. The irony is not lost here, Wallace D. Mohammad broke with *Nation Of Islam* because many aspects of its belief system did not jive with the versions of Islam preserved in Middle Eastern tradition and literature, but that same tradition (and logic) is used by Salafist to classify Wallace as a well-intentioned deviant innovator, whose belief and practices  remove him from the fold of Islam.

In the early 1980s I knew of only two families in my neighborhood who followed Sunni Islam, by today's standards they would not even be considered Muslim. Ten years later much of the male and female population were converted. This is particularly true for the criminal subclass who were retuning home from prison having converted to Sunni Islam. Because the lower classes of Blacks are always in a perpetual state of rebellion they gravitate to ideologies which assume a masculine  posture particularly if it has esoteric aspects and non-mainstream appeal. Street people in turn confer their own legitimacy on whatever movement they embrace.

During the 1990s males in the street from my neighborhood either gravitated to the "lessons" of the 5% Nation,  were Muslims, or followed no spiritual tradition.  Most of us who read books were reading literature from many different 'Islamic' sects like the Moorish Science Temple, Dr. Malachi Z. York's Ansar movement, the Nation of Islam, we also were reading  Black Israelite, Eastern, conspiracy, and  Masonic text.  Nobody I know in the streets professed to be Christian, and the current international gang movement had not yet penetrated American cities and suburbs, there were only local neighborhood gangs. By far the Nation of Islam stood out as  the most serious, organized, and strongest of all the groups with a presence in the "hood."

My impression of the NOI, in my youth, was not one of them being a semi-criminal organization. I have never known  men who were part of  Nation Of Islam to be street criminals; or more precisely, although I have known them to be engaged in organized crime - nefarious schemes like robbery  and murder (even Malcolm X claim the FOI was a violent organization) - I have never known active members of Temples to stand on corners, sell drugs,  pimp, or to frequent night clubs. The members I knew to be in the streets were engaged in robberies and considered selling drugs as "selling poison" to the people. As an adult I understand there were certain elements with the NOI that engaged in all of the above. Nevertheless, this was not the image of themselves that they projected to the public. From the outside looking in they were all consummate professionals.

It should be noted that only particular NOI Temples, out of the tens of thousands of members nationwide, were branded with the criminal stigma. Particularly Temple 25 out of Newark New Jersey, whose members were responsible for the assassination of Malcolm X, and Temple 12 out of Philadelphia, whose members spawned the "Black Mafia." Members from both of these Temples wrestled power away from the Italian Mafia, who at the time, monopolized organized crime in the inner city.

In any event, one reason the NOI no longer have a  large footprint in the prison system is that members of this group do not come to prison. Whereas Sunni Muslims openly engage in all sorts of criminal activity from drug dealing to robbery. It is not unusual to find them in clubs doing all the things that disbelievers do, while still claiming to be strict adherents of  Islam. Well-known gangsters are known to attend their neighborhood mosques.

My first encounter with Sunni Muslims were with the drug dealers who had come home from prison where they learned to read and write Arabic, they were using the Arabic language to graffiti tag their drug sets, this was the only way I knew they were Muslims. The most observant Muslim I knew back then was a local drug dealer whose entire family was run according to strict rules, as far as I could tell he prayed five times a day. We would conduct business and make prayer at his home when it was time. Not all the Muslims were of the criminal element,  but the ones who had the most influence were.

This connection to the criminal subculture is both a blessing and curse. The blessing is that there is no way to instill the masses with righteous morals except through institutions and people they accept as their own. On the other hand the criminal origins of Islam's spread ensures that low breed criminals (of all sort) and drug addiction (of all sort) will have a persistent presence within the community. Therefore the community will suffer stagnation because no complex  organization will occur among this class, only rudimentary institutions will take shape while demoralized  and morally bankrupt  men dominate the ranks.

In fairness it was these men (and women) who were responsible for the spread of the religion on the street level. Back then we were not going to mosques but holding prayers in private homes and project apartments, this is how we learned of rituals like ablution and facing E ast. Likewise, the women were holding taleems or religious meetings in apartments, this is how they learned religion from other women and how to garb themselves. This is the way Christianity spread 2022 years ago; the way Muhammad spread Islam 1443 years ago; and the way that the Garvey movement spread in the 1920s; and the way Fard Muhammad taught his young disciple Elijah Muhammad in the 1930s; and how the Nation of Islam spread in the 1930-1970s. According to my third cousin Abdul Karim Hasan (1931- 2019) our family was converted to the Moorish Science Temple in 1942 through meetings held in private homes, and then they were converted to the NOI in 1955 by none other than Malcolm X through this same process, and eventually followed W. D. Mohammad into Sunni Islam in 1975. Every major movement begins in an intimate setting among friends and family, first the household is changed and then the neighborhood, then the community, and then the nation. The first error of our imagination is thinking everything of importance began as a grand gesture or has majestic origins.

In my opinion young women (street girls) were converting to Islam because they were following the men/males coming home from prison who required their 'girlfriends' be Muslim as a precondition for a serious relationship. Furthermore, Islam more than Christianity held out the real possibility of marriage, being that street level Muslims were the only males who take the concept of marriage seriously. If you saw a married man in the hood most likely he was a Muslim. A young woman could come out of her life of running the streets or even prostitution convert to Islam and find a husband, and be accepted as if she were a chaste virgin. Even now all of the men I know from the neighborhood who are married  with large families are Muslims. And the women they are married to have street origins as themselves.

The reason Black males turned to Islam in prison is that it satisfies many male needs like: fraternity, camaraderie, organization, daily structure, spirituality, intellectual stimulation, protection, and community; this order of importance and need varies from individual to individual. In addition, within the Muslim  community there are always sober and mature men who are willing to guide young men without manipulation or quid pro quo. The young men went into prison learned religion and got new Islamic attributes and when they came home they gave their children Islamic names and their women followed suit. Some men would come home "go straight" and live with their wives according to prescribed rules, they were the people we could look to and observe how Muslims were supposed to behave and dress. In the 1990s we did not know a lot of religion as they seem to know these days, but there was real belief, our criminality did not seem hypocritical.

Even so, the religion has grown much more fundamentalist over the decades. In prison the most conservative and self-righteous Muslims can be violent career-criminals. It is not out of the ordinary to see religiously fanatical men pray and study for a decade (or more), leave prison only to return within a few years after they have sunk back into the underworld and its addictions. Still, it is comical to watch men pay lip service to puritanical religious views while they indulge in all sort of criminal, perverted, and sadistic acts rooted in the most base instincts ever formed in man. To navigate such a world with a straight face is a masterstroke of self-deception.

Many have not waged a war on their lower selves (nafs), but they've submitted to it while redefining what the words righteous and good mean. 'Righteous' and 'good' no longer refer to your actions and proper conduct, it has been divorced from actions. Righteous and good now refers to what you say you believe whether or not you actually live up to it - righteousness is now reduced to a series of verbal formulas. As long as you profess the correct alqidah (belief system) and minhaj you can get away with anything.

These people actually believe that the worst, most evil Muslim with the most correct belief system is better than the person whose behavior is grounded in honorable and honest conduct, but whose belief system is flawed. These men are philosophers of the soul, they love to babble about the heart and purity. They are judges of the unseen who believe they alone, with their deeper understanding of the meaning of the Qur'an and Prophet Muhammad's words, are capable of discerning truth and reality from fiction. I have learned that anybody who wants to discuss the purity of their heart does not want you to know what's on their mind. What can you do but laugh when you see a Salafi/ gangster/gangbanger/ drug dealer/ robber/ drug addict tell someone else he or she is a "deviant" because they read literature from scholars who contradict Salafi dawah (message and teachings).

In the last four decades Sunni Islam has absorbed into its ranks many of the warrior-aged Black males (14-50). Islam has grown by conversion of men and women, proselytizing, family births and foreign immigration. Although I am unable to provide a detailed analysis of the current state of the Salafi Dawah movement as it relates to the African American community nationwide I can only speak of its presence in prison and its reputation in the larger society. I can say that there is a schism between Salafi Muslims and many other Muslim communities; who see Salafi Muslims as rigid, intolerant, and narrow-minded; to the point of being repulsed by their presence in mosques, where they bring their antagonism front and center.

The Salafist, who seem to believe they represent a distinct sect, are always engaged in an ongoing inquisition, and like the Jesuits they would like nothing more than to investigate everyone's beliefs, hunt down deviants, and burn them alive. They relish in exposing people with alleged deficiencies in their belief system, anyone who does not openly declare their fealty to the Salafist minhaj is suspected of heresy. Small-minded fanatical men with long memories are right at home with this strain of Islam. In any case, Salafism and Islam itself may have peaked in zeal and actual influence. Neither has the grip on the minds and hearts of young Black men as it did 20, 30 or 40 years ago.

The older generations are dying and the new generations are not as zealous, militant, or serious as the generations who put Islam on the national map. Once considered exotic, ancient and true, global terrorist organizations have turned people's perception of Islam into a bizarre cult of death hungry sociopaths. In prison it is difficult recruiting mentally stable people seeking spiritual enlightenment. I see far more males disillusioned by gang life turning to Christianity for sanctuary. The Christian ranks have swelled in the last two decades with intelligent Black males trying to find an off ramp from violent gang activity. Groups like ISIS (who profess to be Salafist) and their brief reign of barbarism -  ending in humiliation - have many struggling to make sense of their own belief system. I am told that the backbone of the mosques and Islamic communities are not strong disciplined men but strong and disciplined women.

Although the Nation of Islam has not had a presence in New Jersey Correctional facilities for three decades, I know that it still has a strong presence in the national prison system and can be found in small pockets in many communities. However, in general, the growth of Sunni Islam within the Black community nationwide has eclipsed the NOI organization. Which is a loss, because the Fruit of Islam or FOI (male vanguard) were among the most well disciplined, competent, and informed Black men that I had the privilege to encounter. They also have a unique and healthy historical narrative. The women from this community are jewels, and have no peers in spiritual refinement. I would take a wife who was trained in this community any day of the week. It was the institutions put in place and sacrifices made by the early NOI that laid the foundation for Sunni Islam to flourish in America.

From 1960 through the 1990s the NOI presence in urban areas was a blessing. The men were a visible example of masculine refinement. They could be seen as serial entrepreneurs, even acting as security in criminally infested housing projects, they were highly respected and even feared. They were not the type of Black men you played with. When I was young me and my best friend got our hands on two kufis and would wear them and act like we were Muslims. We would see men and women leaving their Temple gatherings, they were so clean and dignified that you could not take your eyes off them, and  the men were there in force. Even today whenever I see the men, women, and children in their religious attire I am struck with nostalgia  and overwhelming respect.

Unlike church people, members of the Nation were not old with canes or overweight, they looked like soldiers in suits. Even without their suits they could be identified by their posture and alertness. The NOI was synonymous with order and discipline, although few in number, whenever a young friend became a member of the group their change was immediate and substantive, they turned into well-spoken professors overnight. I saw young men who I considered to be apathetic slobs as hustlers in the streets transformed into focused young men in a matter of months. Whenever they spoke you would have to blink a few times to make sure this was the same person.

In any event prison administrations  had no choice but to fold by the sheer force-of-will of Islam and soon became amiable towards Sunni Islam (pre-9/11 and suspicious post 9/11) which allowed it to flourish within penitentiary system. Once it was understood that Islam was here to stay, Muslims were afforded spaces to preach and teach (Muslims put up a fight for these privileges beginning with the NOI throughout the national prison system in the 1950s). Prison administrators soon welcomed the less militant and less organized authority of the Sunni religious structure, one man controlling so many made their job easier. Sunni Islam was a welcomed replacement to the NOI which was considered too militant and too Black nationalist.

Most of the old guard in these communities were originally adherents to the NOI and still harbor Black nationalist sentiments, but kept quiet while the new order of Sunni Islam was ushered in, first with Wallace D. Mohammad who presented a mainstream version of Islam to the world, then with more orthodox forms of Islam which looked to Middle Eastern (Saudi-Arabian) scholars and literature for guidance in religion. The result was the cultivation of a generation of Black men who were without racial consciousness or politics. Raising Black people from the dead by fulfilling their spiritual, intellectual, economic, and material needs was no longer the focus. This new Islamic identity only allows for the world to be divided between "believers" and "disbelievers," while their focus is aimed exclusively on establishing  Sunni Mosques, preparation for the "the afterlife," and worldly Jihad.

In prison Muslims are even discouraged from showing solidarity with other groups in fighting for social rights. They are taught that Muslim problems are separate from everyone else, membership to social groups like the NAACP and the like is criticized. Even prison food strikes and protest for better conditions by the masses are often ignored. Muslims are taught to view participation in the politkal process itself  as anti-Islamic; within popular interpretations of the religion Constitutional Rights, Voting, and Democracy are dismissed  as being for disbelievers.

If sharia law or the Islamic State does not exist on earth then all institutions are considered illegitimate. If it does not effect the Islamic community directly believers are warned against cooperating with the masses. There is a powerful strain of fatalism that rules the minds, everything is classified as "god's will," even before initiative to change the circumstances has occurred. The Islam being propagated is heavy in monasticism, every male is encouraged to model their behavior after 7th century warrior monks.

This self separatism  creates tension between the leadership and the larger Islamic community who see their plight as linked with the oppressed of any color. The leadership who want to be segregated and cultish,  cherry pick verses and traditions they need to justify their position, while those at the bottom believe their religion is personal and want to throw their hat in with all people who want social change - no matter their belief. Within this paradigm the American (global) reality of racial, class, and caste politics creates a tension within Black "believers." What he is told the truth is by some of his leaders does not match what his eyes see or what physical reality imposes on his sense.

Islam tells the believer that: *'Your skin and your status does not matter and should not be factored into your thinking at all.'* But the reality is that ALL of the most powerful institutions and governments in the world (including the Islamic ones) are organized by a highly visible racial, ethnic, or tribal hierarchy. And this fact is not lost on  any Black person, no matter their class.

The bottom line is that the masses of Muslims don't want to separate themselves from their brothers and sisters or from the rest of humanity for that matter, and will resist interpretations of religious doctrine that forces this upon them. Most Muslims want to practice their religion in freedom and call  humanity to the faith. They don't want to fight against other Muslims and investigate their belief system.

A lot of what is taught in prison as being from the Islamic tradition is in fact only conclusions of barely literate men, interpreting the religion the way they see fit; they base their conclusions on a few books they have read that have been translated into English from Arabic. In prison the men teach and memorize from books which conform to a particular school of thought. The answers to life  are deduced from reading people's favorite scholars. The prison leadership are often fanatic pseudo-intellectuals who have little experience practicing the religion in the real world. When truly learned men - trained in Islamic Universities - enter their presence it never fails to produce animosity.

# THE PARADOX OF MORE BOOKS
# AND LESS KNOWLEDGE

In two decades of observation I have noticed a very strange paradox when it comes to describing the different personality types produced under the guidance of the Nation Of Islam, vis a' vis the orthodox Sunni Islamic tradition. Males raised within the Fruit Of Islam and the Warithudeen community that followed had a broad range of knowledge about various subjects, following the lead of Malcolm X who helped organize this group of men and women, the FOI (Women were MGT) were required to study not only their own religious literature like the *Qur'an, Message to the Black man & Our savior has arrived,* but universal history, sociology, mathematics, rhetoric, law, business, martial arts and anything that would help strengthen their community, prove the truth of their faith, and raise them out of the slave mentality of fear and dependence. Martial arts was mandatory for all males entering the NOI in the later years. The knowledge they acquired was used to advance them in business, discipline, and unity. Resurrecting the mentally and spiritually dead Black person was their agenda and their personalities, business model, and institutions reflected this vision.

They were invested in the community and established very effective methods to reach back down to the worst drug addicted and criminal types to pull them out of their pitiful state. These men saw themselves as being the living examples of refinement and were sympathetic towards Black men and women (their brothers and sisters) who had sunken into the pits of despair and resorted to addiction, drug dealing, robbery, or prostitution to cope with life. Those at the bottom were to be uplifted out of their state by any means necessary. The philosophical mission of the Nation Of Islam gave/ gives them a zeal and thirst for knowledge which turned them into exceptionally well-read men and women, who could be integrated into any existing institution. The early success of Sunni Islam is a direct result of generations of men and women having undergone disciplined training within the Nation of Islam's rigorous male (FOI) and female (MGT/ &  GCC) institutions, before being converted to orthodox Islam. They were driven by the belief that they were civilizing the world beginning with Black people.  They were truly the seeds to Islam's rise in Black America

 Whereas although Sunni Muslims have far more access to "authentic" Islamic literature and their depth of knowledge of Islamic traditions is deeper, their breadth of secular knowledge and understanding of worldly affairs is more narrow. When they study it is primarily Islamic material approved of (authenticated) by their respective schools of thought. As a consequence, I find that the more Arabianized Sunni Islam becomes, the more intellectually underdeveloped individuals are produced. The Strict interpretations of Islam emanating from Saudi Arabia and Europe are suited for producing slavish men with a fixation for intolerance, oppression of women, hate of Jews, and death- they love rules which restrict human behavior, expression, and creativity. They think governing or ruling over people means interrogating them about the intricacies of their belief system.

Many are not acquiring the intellectual tools suited for thriving in a free and open Western-style society, with diverse populations rooted in religious tolerance. America's tradition of liberal philosophical inquiry and individualism (free thinking and disagreement-but cooperation) is antithetical to the world view being developed in the Sunni Islamic stratosphere of prison; where deviant ideas are even less tolerated than deviant behavior.

These men claim to have the best ideas on how to govern and rule over everyone but yet are afraid to put their beliefs to the test in open debate. In this society ideas are subject to challenge and if your truth cannot stand up to the scrutiny and rigor of scientific and historic investigation then you are in no position to assume the posture of a competent authority, let alone intellectual arrogance. More to the point you cannot be ready to impose your ideas on the entire world but yet evade debate about miscellaneous concepts surrounding your belief.

I am not saying that this is Islam, I am saying that this is the version of Islam being taught to Black men in prison and in turn, finding its way into African American communities. Islam is a very diverse global religion with long tradition and voluminous literature which spans fifteen centuries; it has many expressions and every land, community, region, and era the religion enters alters the way the faith looks; even so, the men I encounter have a narrow and shallow view of Islam and even shallower intellectual depth. They are simply out of their league when it comes to independent analytical thought, mastery of different disciplines, and methodological inquiry.

To the point, when the conversation ventures outside of the bounds of anything not described by Islamic tradition, law, history, logic or reality they are at a loss for words. If they have not been told how to think or what to think on a matter they cannot form an opinion, and are afraid to do so out of fear of transgressing the bounds of 'Islamic Knowledge;' subjects that seemingly conflict with Islamic reality are simply avoided altogether; a fear of secular knowledge permeates the Sunni community in prison. I have spoken to many non-Muslim intellectuals who consider Sunni Muslims to be weak in intellect because they steer clear of and avoid debate on a broad range of topics.

I know for a fact that young Muslims are told NOT to read a lot of books out of fear that they will become confused on matters of faith and inadvertently turned into deviant thinkers. It is truly a sight to behold, men with rooms full of scholarly books which cost hundreds and thousands of dollars, but on close examination their minds are not broadened but intentionally confined to repetitive curriculum meant to restrict their psychological horizon. Interestingly, I find Muslims who read a diverse range of Islamic literature have a broader outlook about the religion, are far less rigid in their interpretation of the Qur'an and Sunna and are more open minded in Islam's application in the modern world.

Furthermore, Sunni Muslims don't aggressively proselytize or seek out converts, rather they condescendingly hold all non-Muslims (Black, white or other) in disdain and consider them to be physically filthy "kafirs" (disbelievers). Disbelievers (who are often more honest and have better characters than Muslims) are seen as potential enemies. Befriending, helping, or assisting them is heavily criticized. The drug addicted, gang bangers, and criminal-minded are not to be helped but avoided like lepers. They are not viewed as misguided young men and women with the potential for greatness, but enemies who will corrupt you if you get too close to them.

This attitude has its own consequences, the masses of disbelievers in prison have grown to detest Muslims as hypocrites. The widespread criminal conduct and drug abuse of Muslims also contributes to this opinion. I have been the fly on the wall in many gatherings and listen to the opinions of Non-Muslims, they don't respect Muslims, rather they fear them like they fear any other group of men who are organized enough to inflict violence. It is common for non-Muslims to refer to Muslims as "fake ass Muslims" or "just another gang."

To hear Islamic sermons in prison where Black nationalism is mocked as that "Black man crap" is not unusual (only Black Imams do this). However, this does not play well with the crowd who don't like Black Imams talking down about Muhammad Ali, the NOI, or Black nationalism. Black people don't want to hate other people and welcome converts of all colors, but neither will they allow their heritage to be bashed. In order to prove their purity in thought, Black imams distance themselves from racial politics and have an acute aversion to anything African although there are many African Muslims.

In fact there was essentially an Arabcentric (Saudi) world view that took hold of many African American ummah (religious communities). African American Muslims are actually not informed about the geo-politkal realities of Islamic countries in the Middle East, Africa, Asia, China or Europe nor do they understand the complexity of the internal politics of these countries, rather they are particularly indoctrinated to see these places with rose colored glasses and focus their empathy toward Arabcentric political affairs, tremendous deference is afforded foreign opinions on all matters of religion.

I have seen faces turn in disgust at the mere mention of Africa yet the turmoil in the Middle East or Asia  is always against 'the brothers' who are always portrayed as victims of "the West". When the Taliban seized power in Afghanistan in 2021 there was actually optimism about the "Brothers" doing "good." When I heard this I laughed  at the childlike thought process. Despite what they say no one I know (Muslim or not) would ever want to live in the world of the Taliban, let alone survive under such conditions.

In prison Black Imams refuse to address issues concerning Black people, who comprise upward of 95% of their ranks. They refuse to concentrate on that "Black man crap," because in their mind they are above race issues. Black people are only considered/ mentioned or viewed as a whole when their flaws are being criticized; Black moral failure (inferior traits) is a favorite topic of Black Muslims, outside of this context Blacks are seen as individuals. I have heard many Khutbahs (Friday sermons) where Blackness (as a people) is denied as having any religious relevance what-so-ever and the next week the same speakers rails on about the moral decay of the "Black people" in the "hood," who are now considered a single entity.

In this new Islam, Black people, as a whole, are not recognized for good things but they can be recognized for their bad things. Under this Islamic order Black identity is sacrificed to achieve purity of ideology, although the ethnic identity and pride of foreign born Muslims is never asked to be extinguished. Foreign born Imams are not afraid to mention  the sad ratio of Black faces staring at them in prisons.

This de-racialized religion is the Islam that spread from prison to prison and is the  strain of Islam men returned home with back into their communities. I first encountered this thinking in the 1990s, when I mentioned something pertaining "Black people" to my sheikh and he rebutted with: "So what." As if to  say: 'what does that Black issue have to do with me?' I had always looked at life through a Black male's gaze, 'Black  power' was in the music, culture,  art, and literature. My teacher's comment left me confused but not convinced.

This was not just a prison phenomenon this perspective was/is being cultivated wherever Sunni Muslims are found and that is in many major cities. It seems that too many Blacks are led to believe that they must forfeit their heritage in order to be accepted into the global 'brotherhood' when it is not even required. Islam only requires the belief that all humans are equal. It does not mean your tribe, or ethnicity (and the politics associated with it) disappear once you accept the faith.

It is my belief that any attempt to divorce the religion from the Black American historical / sociopolitical reality will backfire. It is not going to work because it is the lower class Blacks who confer legitimacy on ideologies, once you lose them you have lost legitimacy in the eyes of the people, Islam is no different. Once it begins to take on a mainstream appeal or neutral posture or have no place for "Black identity" it will be rejected. I have heard many rank and file members say openly *"do these niggahs think they Arabs"*? Black people don't dislike Arabs, they simply don't want to  be the suckers of Anglo Saxons, Jews, or Arabs who they understand to have financial and organizational advantage, and their own political agenda.

The larger point being made is that leaders matter, ideas matter, and world-view matters. The philosophical diet that the people are being fed will effect their behavior and their prospects for survival. What the people believe must effect how they express themselves individually as well as collectively. I was able to reflect on over three decades of local history in and outside of prison and document the drastic shift in psychology, attitude, and behavior of the males I observed and trace it directly to the change in religious belief. Although we recoil from celebrations of Black pride as narrow-minded and out of step with  the times, we must admit the evidence that it is a supreme motivator is undeniable.

*********

Blacks in America don't seem to be able to stay sufficiently motivated without there being a component of collective elevation involved in the plan. If Black people are not busy organizing, building, and dying for our united destiny then we simply die for other people's causes or chasing materialism. While we long for a unified cause our leaders keep us busy working for a utopia where we are integrated with everyone in the world except ourselves. Consider the following excerpts from The Autobiography of Malcolm X  written by Alex Haley.

**Haley:** "You may have read somewhere – a lot has been written concerning it- about the Nation of Islam's phenomenal record of dope-addiction cures of longtime junkies. In fact, the New York Times carried a story about how some of the social agencies have asked representatives of the Muslim program for clinical suggestions.

**Malcolm X:** The Muslim program began with recognizing that color and addiction have a distinct connection. It is no accident that in the entire Western Hemisphere, the greatest localized concentration of addicts in Harlem.

*Our cure program's first major ingredient was the painfully patient work of Muslims who previously were junkies themselves. In the ghetto's dope jungle, the Muslim ex-junkies would fish out addicts who knew them back in those days. Then with an agonizing patience that might span anywhere from a few months to a year, our ex-junky Muslims would conduct the addicts through the Muslim six-point therapeutic process........*

*When the addict's withdrawal sets in, and he is screaming, cursing, and begging, "Just one shot, man!" the Muslims are right there talking junkie jargon to him. "Baby, knock that monkey off your back! Kick that habit! Kick Whitey off your back!" The addict, writhing in pain, his nose and eyes running, is pouring sweat from head to foot. He's trying to knock his head against the wall, flailing his arms, trying to fight his attendants, he is vomiting suffering diarrhea. "Don't hold nothing back! Let Whitey go, baby!" You're going to stand tall, man! I can see you now in the Fruit of Islam!"*

*When the awful ordeal is ended, when the grip of dope is broken, the Muslims comfort the weak ex-addict, feeding him soups and broths, to get him on his feet again. He will never forget these brothers who stood by him during this time. He will never forget that it was the Nation of Islam's program which rescued him from the special hell of dope. And that black brother (or sister, whom Muslim sisters attend) rarely ever will return to the use of narcotics. Instead, the ex-addict when he is proud clean, renewed, can scarcely wait to hit the same junky jungle he was in, to "fish" out some buddy and salvage him!" 16*

This is only an edited passage, the original is much more touching, when I first read this in the Autobiography Of Malcolm X in 2021 I burst into tears and could not stop. I had never heard of anything like this. I had heard stories of the Nation of Islam getting Black men off of heroin and lifting them out of their horrible situation, but thought they were just anecdotes I never knew this was an entire program that had steps to it or that the process could take up to a year.

I am 43 years old and I have never been part of, nor have I ever witnessed another religious organization with that much love and belief in Black men. Our predecessors did not have to look toward the Middle East to solve their modern problems, they understood our people and set out to change them from the root. Somehow we have gotten off course, imagine looking at a filthy black man or woman in the gutter today with tracks and sores on their arm and seeing them one day named after one the attributes of god. Today men and women that have not even sunken this low are written off as hopeless cases. Our religions are ruled, populated by, and cultivate Pharisees.

Finally I will bring home my point that ideas and philosophy matter. Consider the assets accumulated by the Nation Of Islam during the "First Resurrection" while it was being led by a man with a 4$^{th}$ grade education. The sheer scope of their accomplishments is a testament to the organization's drive and business acumen. These people were not playing lip service to the idea of lifting the Black man out of dependency. According to author Abdul Karim Hasan he was selected by W. D. Mohammad to assemble a team to take inventory of the Nation Of Islam's assets after the death of Elijah Muhammad. In his book *Our Family's Evolution from Nationalism to Al-Islam*, Abdul Karim Hasan catalogs the scope of the various assets and holding in an impressive list. *According to Karim Hasan, Elijah Muhammad's Estimated holdings in Chicago alone amounted to near 100,000,000. Hasan Karim in his inventory says this list only represents part of what was found, recorded and reported:*

Farm Land: 9000 acres in Alabama producing beans, corn, wheat, cotton, vegetables, and watermelons. Over a three-year period, we harvested and transported 1,240,00 pounds of watermelons from 5.000 acres in Georgia.

Main crops: Soybean, corn, hay, and a beef herd of eight-hundred head. An ultra-modern dairy with two herds of milking cows, as well as a cannery and 1,000 acres of land in Michigan.

Main Crops: corn, fifty acres of apple orchards, two huge silos with a 100,000 bushel's capacity, storage bin: two house egg factory containing 40,000 chickens, a dairy herd of one hundred milking cows and Holstein cows.

Progressive Land Developers was a holding company that held title to most of the Nation's property-grocery stores, supermarkets, fast food shops, first class three hundred capacity Salaam restaurants, clothing stores, coffee shops, and bakeries.

Fish markets (cooked and uncooked), and newly built three story sales and Office building, on Stoney Island in Chicago.

The Nation's Bank, The Guaranty National Bank Recapitalization- I met with State banking authorities several times.

American Punch Food- M.R.E.- Plant.

23,000,000 contract from President Carter's Government

University of Islam  School Building

Muslim Import store

Muhammad Import warehouse containing imports from Japan: watches, pots and pans, clothes, household goods, fabric, luggage, tableware, dishes, and utensils.

The National Clothing Factory, containing uniforms and streetwear for women.

Several Dry Cleaning Plants,

Our Truck Fleet, which included three brand new Kenworth tractor & trailer trucks, two brand new Peterbilt tractor and trailer, and one brand new International tractor and trailer truck

One B-24 Cargo Plane (that crashed on landing)

One Lear Passenger Jet (sold for 2,000,000).

Muhammad Speaks Newspaper's brand new $2,000,000 printing press and 60,000 square feet newspaper plant.

Chicago Lamb Packer Slaughter House, where our meats were slaughtered and prepared for shipping. 17

Karim says there were "over two hundred homes and units of housing for over eight hundred people in Chicago. Farming equipment and equipment that if lined up end to end would stretch nearly three miles." In addition to this there was a vast network of national Temple mosques incorporated under Elijah Muhammad's Leadership and attached to them were restaurants; there was as well as 3,000,000 in cash in the #2 Poor Treasury Bank account; and a 4,400,000 church building  that was purchased with the help of Libyan president Muammar Qadafi. These were not just random holdings but an entire infrastructure with a centralized chain of command.

This list is not just the celebration of "dunya" (worldly) material achievement, but further proof of superior organization and command of logistical capabilities. The men and women had structured  paramilitary chain of command and were organized according to ranks, titles, positions of responsibility, and respect. When they carried out their duties with efficiency they were elevated and given greater responsibility, and when they proved incapable or incompetent they were removed from their post (often punished) and replaced for good cause and with due procedure.  Such a feat would have made Marcus Garvey proud.

The Temples national educational system was churning out dedicated  and refined soldiers, men and women who were the cream of the crop in their respective communities. When people speak of The "Honorable" Elijah Muhammad I'm not sure if they are really encompassing the scope and gravity of what he was able to accomplish in forty years and what was lost at his death. This was for all-intents-and-purposes the embryonic stage of a functioning Black government - a nation within a nation. According to Malcolm X when he came home from prison in 1952 there were no more than 400 members of the NOI and many of them were old people, before his death in February 1965 he estimated the Nation of Islam membership to be 40,000. According to Nafeesa Muhammad the Nation of Islam's economic program (1934-1975) peaked in the late 1960s and early 1970s with an estimated 250,000 active members worldwide in 1975.

Malcolm X said of this organization that he helped build *"We had the best organization the black man's ever had - niggers ruined it!"* Malcolm 's criticism came when he was on the outs and probably being hunted down by members of the Nation, so his comment suggest not only understandable resentment but naiveté, in that he did not fully appreciate the process and the growing pains that come with new religious movements and power. There is chaos in the beginning stages of any religion. Consider the Hebrew revolution in law and order under Moses and the early leaders of Judaism. The Exodus and the early decades (40 years in the wilderness) of the founding of the Jewish people saw a multitude of stateless people, with no previous experience in governing themselves as a nation, war against other nations and themselves.

The great tribulations of the early centuries of the church is well known, the first 400 years of Christianity the community was a minority sect being persecuted by Roman aristocratic pagans, the next 1,000 years was riddled with conquest, infighting, sectarian wars, and political turmoil. Western Christianity has only been civilized within the last 300 years, after going through the European Enlightenment and being  domesticated by strong secular administrative States and capitalism.

The early Muslim community in the first decade of the prophet Muhammad's call to Islam saw the persecution of believers by Arabia's pagans, and the social upheavals of the Muslim world after Muhammad's death are well documented, three out of the first four Caliphs (rulers) were murdered along with many members of the Prophet's family. Sunni Islam is still in a state of sectarian infighting. In summary, wherever there are men, power, titles, and money at stake there will be fighting and bloodshed. The Nation of Islam was no different, they were stricken with the same diseases that all religions experience in the beginning stages of their mission.

***

Fast forward 50 years after the fact, the present Sunni Muslim community is more numerous, have more collective wealth, more diverse, educated, and traveled. Nevertheless, apart from W. D. Muhammad I cannot recall one African American Sunni Imam who is a nationally recognized figure or who has forged a comparable record of achievement for his community from such lowly beginnings. Nor any who has amassed such material holdings for his community or that has established a national chain of Mosques or a national curriculum that produces ideologically standardized young men and women.

The Sunni community of W.D. Muhammad has truly inherited the positive aspects of the NOI and combined them with an authentic Islamic tradition. W.D. Muhammed succeeded in establishing a highly competent Islamic community with international reach. One that was able to thrive and maintain its identity and course after his death.

This community has a national network of businesses, schools and mosques, and a membership comprised of many Black professionals. Men and women from this community are scholarly proficient in the arts of Qur'anic recitation and interpretation, and adept in sciences of Islamic jurisprudence. Which is applied to their own native landscape. Furthermore, their practical interpretation of the Qur'an and Sunnah make them well suited to integrate and thrive in American society.

Unfortunately for this community, faux fundamentalism has captured the minds and hearts of lower class Black males, who regard W.D. Muhammad and his followers as "deviants"; this absurd ideological posture ensures that (in certain regions) cooperation and recruitment from this segment of society remains a challenge.

In prison and I suspect elsewhere the organizational structure of Black Sunni Muslims is rudimentary or non existent. I have never heard of any centralized body of Muslim men and women that have binding authority in regional or  geographical religious affairs. Every man who has acquired knowledge, respect, and authority has no authority over any other Muslim community outside of those in his own flock who  have submitted to his authority.

Although war and jihad are common themes in the Sunni tradition  I have never heard of any Sunni para-military institutions being cultivated on American soil;  if these exist they are completely clandestine. It seems that if the tradition does not explicitly tell the men what to do they are unable conjure it from imagination or necessity. To form such ranks does not constitute innovation in religion, the early Islamic communities had basic forms of hierarchy, including governors, wakils, wazirs etc.

In any case, Prison still produces its fair share of militant intellectual Black men, only their energies are focused towards different goals. Instead of a struggle against the State or devising plans for collective community development, too many Black males have been locked into a spiritual (cosmic) battle to save their soul, and little else matters to them. I see little evidence that he is actually winning his battle. From these ranks no future Malcolm X like figures can arise because the men are not being cultivated or instructed to go home and save their families, neighborhoods, communities and nation.

Rather they are filled with fantasies of fighting Jihad in foreign lands with a harem of exotic obedient wives  while they build a utopian State based on Sharia law.  For clarification, New Jersey's prison system is by no means producing  Black "radicalized " Muslims.  Instead they are churning out legions of males who pay lip service to Conservative Islamic positions on matters of Qur'anic interpretation and implementation. I, for one, do not take them seriously because I am close enough to see through this thick veneer of religion that covers their actions.

This is a man who can come home see the carnage that drugs has cost 'his people,' see the misguided young men creating anarchy, see drug dealers, and prostitutes in his vicinity and raise his family and children in this environment without qualms. Although he is perfectly suited to transform the environment he knows best he never comes to the realization  that he should be an agent of change where he is needed most.

Meanwhile the drug dealer and gang banger can sit in prison and fantasize about the plan he has for this same neighborhood, he cannot wait to  come home and turn his "hood" into an extension of his warped criminal hedonistic fantasy. He cannot wait to arrive like a king to take, conquer, manipulate, exploit and  execute his plans with as much violence and fun as necessary.  In these two scenarios ten Muslims of similar attitude and disposition occupied with daydreams of  "overseas" adventure do not exert the force and influence over a neighborhood that one gangster does - imagine that. The gangster's religion is actually more potent in this case.

If the males are no longer finding positive stimulation through Islam where are they going, where is their militant energy being used? This turns us to the next subject of the IGM or International Gang Movement. This is a phrase I coined to describe the unprecedented  Black Gang culture that has proliferated internationally within the last 25 years.

# NOTE

For this essay I have gone out of my way to consult current and former gang members whose experience and knowledge of the culture is invaluable. Furthermore, I myself have watched this movement from the sidelines for over 22 years. I have lived around gang members through most of my time in prison and some of my friends and associates are, former or current, members whose intellect and opinions I respect.

## INTERNATIONAL GANG MOVEMENT

If I were to identify another phenomenon responsible for Black males' loss of political (militant)  and racial consciousness, within and outside the prison system, I would have to point to the tsunami of gang culture that swept Black communities nationwide. Gangs have amassed considerable cultural clout in the last 25 years. No longer branded as just criminals, they are presented in mainstream pop culture as an extension of urban America. Rappers and sports figures (millionaires) openly discuss their gang affiliations, wear their colors and throw up gang signs without any commercial repercussions. At Super Bowl 56 in 2022 Snoop Dogg, who began as a West coast gangster rapper, but has now transcend to become an icon of  mainstream American pop culture,  performed the "Crip walk" (or dance) in front of an audience of a 50,000,000. The Crip walk is a well known dance associated with West coast Crips, one of the most violent street gangs in America that has many sets. Even if his dance did not advocate gangbanging it certainly legitimized it on the international stage. Snoop Dogg says openly he is not an active gang member, nonetheless, his antics celebrate and commercialize gang culture not denounce it. If all they do is  a silly little dance they can't be that bad, right?

Gang members have their own dress codes, speech, language, music (music labels, dances, videos, and albums), web sites histories and ideology. They are unapologetically criminal minded, and the only thing that matters is money, power, and respect (for me and my set).  Racial consciousness is primarily subverted because gang identity takes precedence over racial identity. In the end, positive cultural identity is wiped out as the generations embrace nihilism and complete amorality.

Gangs which are real criminal networks hit every state,  city and neighborhood differently. Black males are coming to prison, or leaving prison initiated into gangs. These are not  the local gangs that have always been present in neighborhoods, but gangs that have grown into transnational and international organizations with regional sets and mainstream recognition. The fact that members move around the country under the same brand and franchise and have members in different countries makes them international - in form not in substance. Young males from all over the country are now running  to California and New York, among other places, to check in and establish ties with the leaders of their respective sets.

The two institutions with organic organizational power in the inner cities have both been dismal failures in terms of organizing the Black male and his environment. The Black church  has little presence in the life of Black males except for a monopoly over their funeral rites; while Islam failed to cure the issues plaguing the Black male in his American habitat. For that reason and many others their ranks have been decimated from gang conversion. Black males have left Islam en masse to join gangs, others have never given up their criminal ways after accepting the faith. Those who have not left in body have left in spirit. It is quite telling how many young gang bangers born to Muslim families in the 80s and 90s come to prison with Islamic names. Many coming  from families and neighborhoods that have been Muslim for one or two generations.

The rise of gang membership has left legions of Black males who feel no sense of  obligation to their own neighborhoods, communities, or the Black collective self (the 5% Nation was also decimated from gang conversion). The collective "we" as it pertains to the Black people is weakened by fraternal loyalty. To say "we" in reference to Black people in a positive light brings strange looks or laughs,  and makes  some Black males uncomfortable. To think of ourselves as having a common interest is  as silly and amusing to them as the belief in one God is to a polytheist. This conversation is not easy to have with the younger generation, who may look at you sideways if the words 'The Sistas' comes out of your mouth.

In fairness, political consciousness is something that ebbs and flows in society in general. It was around 2005 when I first began to take notice that political awareness was wiped out of young Black males, gang politics had become everything. The circulation of revolutionary and afrocentric  literature was at an all time low. The use of terms like 'the Sistas' caused disconnect and confusion. The use of "Black woman" had no positive emotional connotation. Black women were not seen as our sacred mothers whose honor is worthy of protection. The Black women were no longer an entity whose struggle and experience must be placed and understood in historical context.  She was like the rest of women whose emotional life was irrelevant. She was/ is nothing but a sexual object whose anatomy, flexibility, and potential for exploitation is of primary interest.  She is reduced to one of two categories:  pretty or ugly.

I noticed that the Black woman was not special to this generation of males, sometimes she meant nothing to them. This generation of males treat mothers like no generation of Black males in world history. The Black woman is actually considered lower than other women in this respect; she rarely if ever fits into the category of  exotic beauty which young males are indoctrinated to believe represent the highest concept of beautiful. White women have even come down a notch, now it is the Latina or the racially ambiguous / Brazilian type who are considered the most attractive. Just as Tupac predicted we have a *"race of babies who hate the ladies that make the babies."*

When I was growing up the use of endearing terms like "the Sistas" meant that I, as a Black male, had to think empathetically about the Black women's experience. What were her struggles; how was she experiencing the world; what abuse or cruelties has she experienced; what pain has she felt and what have I contributed to her problems; what harms have I inflicted on her; what were her duties and obligations towards me; and what were my obligations towards her? I was called on to reflect on how I have (or not) carried out my obligations to my family.

Terms like 'Black man', 'brotha' and 'sista' are endearing. To call someone 'Black man' means *'I see you and recognize you as a man even if no one else will.'* It means you must do everything in your power to earn that title. Terms like 'Sista' and 'Brotha' are common terms for people who see themselves as part of the same community, or formally oppressed people who have come through a revolutionary moment in history and emerged as survivors. When people have been through a terrible experience together, class or superficial differences disappear, and they see only brothers and sisters; hence 'brother' and 'sister' are how they address one another. Such terms are laughed at these days and have no context wherein they seem appropriate. I do not entirely fault the gang movement for such a drastic shift in perspective, but, the decline of such vocabulary words coincides with the rise of gang culture and its focus on conflict, fratricide, and hedonism.

I did not see a mass-scale shift in political awareness until the death of Travon Martin in 2012, when the media, unable to cover up the story, pushed nonstop coverage of the tragedy. Travon Martin's death woke the entire Black populous up from its slumber and caused us to take stock of our surroundings. People who were talking their "post racial" spiel were forced into silence. Those who said it was "just about class" were forced to retract their statements. I consider this to be a form of pseudo-consciousness because it is media manufactured, and entirely a result of being inundated with media images and nonstop commentary of Black victimhood. This is similar to being "woke." As opposed to the self-enlightenment  that occurs when an individual, class, or population sets out to transform their spirit and environment by acquiring  and applying knowledge.

In any event,  according to many sources, when gang culture began to spread, their message was that they were starting  the movement with "revolutionary" ideals in mind. I witnessed early recruiting in New Jersey and would hear the gang recruiters (who were my peers) pitching to prospective members that: they were "brothers" forming to "fight against oppression." Story is that they began in 1993 as an oppressed group of Black males within Rikers Island who were resisting the persecution of Latino gangs (Latin Kings and Nietas). Young males were being taught that 'B.L.O.O.D.' was an acronym for: "Brotherly Love Overriding Oppression and Destruction."  I was informed that many of the early members and organizers were 5 % Nation and Muslims which would be consistent with the era and the environment of New York. Their mission statement was to fight against oppression (they even trace their origins to a schism within the Black Panther Party).

I was informed by a veteran gang leader that in the early 1990s when the New York Blood gangs first formed in  New Jersey that they did *indeed* have a curriculum based on revolutionary teachings. And that he had entered the movement because he was told they were "fighting against the system." He said he and others who organized the first New Jersey sets were inspired by the Black Panther Party's militant and charitable platform and their intentions were honorable, but power corrupted the leaders. In addition to the gangs being infiltrated by plants and informants whose job it was to sow sedition and division. When I mentioned the subject of the gang's revolutionary teachings to a young affiliated member fifteen years after I first heard it used, he chuckled and said: "*Oh yeah, did they really believe that [we had righteous goals and origins]?*" He had never heard of such nonsense even though he started banging in the streets in 2006. Furthermore, I am not sure that linking the gang with a revolutionary movement was a selling point or invented mythology to give gangs righteous beginnings - which is a common occurrence. Whatever,  if any, righteous or revolutionary origins were there in the beginning were quickly lost as the gang soon turned into a criminal enterprise.

Although New York Blood sets can now be found throughout the country they have totally different origin than their Los Angeles counterparts. According to a reputable gang leader there was only one LA Blood set (Piru) established in New Jersey around 1991, but other dispute this, claiming the first was another set (DI). I cannot confirm one way or another. I personally first heard references to "Bloods" in New York Hip Hop around 1996 or 1997 by Rap groups ONYX and Capone and Noreaga. ONYX's album The *Last Dayz* made a reference: *"shout out to all my Bloods"* and Capone & Noreaga's album *The War Report*: *"I know you Blood Dun, but read Koran"*.

Such references went over my head because that movement had not found its way to my town. I listened to these albums religiously on the streets, yet had no idea that there was a new gang spreading. Furthermore, in 1995-96 I spent time in the youth correctional facilities with young males from throughout the state and never heard any of them rep this new gang. As far as I was concerned, hardcore rapper Tim Dog said: "Fuck Compton" in 1991 and ridiculed the whole Blood and Crip war as being some dumb shit, and that's pretty much how I felt. I first heard of Bloods in New Jersey in 2001 from a State prisoner who had come back to the county jail from a maximum security prison. I also first encountered actual Bloods in 2001 in Albert C. Wagner Correctional facility, they were small in number but the movement had all the momentum.

On the street I only knew two people who were alleged to be Crip, one who moved from California and did not talk about his past or gangs, the other was rumored to be Crip, but he was not a hustler so I never paid much attention to him. I did not meet another person who claimed Crip until 2007, by this time I had been in the prison system for eight years. It was not that there were no Crips around,  it was that they were not in sufficient number, so they remained incognito. As gangs go - through numbers alone - Blood dominated  the prison system for over a decade, their worst enemy was themselves.

It was in 2001 that I began to observe them and listen to their message. The shift in self perception becomes evident considering how the nicknames of criminals changed after the gang movement came on the scene. It was Islam, Afrocentrism, and  the 5% Nation that first caused young men to take on African names, Islamic or righteous attributes. For three decades males  influenced by Afrocentricity legally changed their names to Swahili names, while those part of the 5% Nation of Gods & Earths were referring to themselves as: *Justice, Understanding, Allah, Knowledge born, King sun, Sun god, Righteous, or Mathematics etc,* and the Islamic names ran the spectrum of Allah's 99 attributes. I myself consulted a book with Allah's 99 beautiful  names when I chose the attribute Salaam for my self in 1997, it was meant to denote the 'Bringer of Peace.' The most diabolical names back then were mafia inspired nicknames like Gotti, Gambino, Capone, and Nitty etc.

However, with the introduction of the gangs to the national culture, the nicknames of criminals changed. Dark, ominous,  and even evil monikers became more prevalent.  In my first personal encounter with a Blood member he introduced himself as "Bloody Bloodthurst", once I realized he wasn't joking, I thought it was some silly shit for little kids. So my first impression of this movement was that it was some corny niggaz who wanna be crazy, and that they were trouble makers. These names demonstrate that a new spirit had taken hold of the Black male imagination. Suddenly, in the early 2000s, I would hear males calling themselves "Bloody" this, "Killah" that, "Homicide", "Murder", "Red Rum." The names "Murder" and Killah are used so frequently that those who use them need another name to go along with it just to tell them apart. Killah Rah, Killah Black, etc.

The absurdity of the new monikers is endless, males have resorted to naming themselves the most evil names and assuming very dark personas. If this christening process suggest that males are not simply caught in a cycle of violence and ignorance, but have fully embraced it as their permanent way of life. In my opinion, taking on an evil name and tattooing yourself on the face,  convey the same message: *Look at me, this person I have become is my new dark self, there is no turning back for me!*

With the rise of gang culture came yet another shift in collective perception. Cities that were gang capitals were elevated to sacred cites, American cities with the most infamy and the highest murder rate became revered places. The cities, neighborhoods, or streets that gangs trace their name and origin became spiritual capitals. The clothes and slang of these places became the new style and lingo and the culture they identified with was emulated. Mecca, Medina, and Jerusalem are no longer holy places, young males turn their faces and hearts to Compton and Chicago for inspiration. It is here they make Hajj, and pay homage to their revered OGs. Like the religious pilgrims who have visited their religious holy land, gang members who have gone to the gang capitals and met with their local "homies" claim  a special status, connection, and legitimacy to the gang.

From the year 2000 to 2010 gang membership exploded nationwide. In the 2000s I witnessed gangs go from a small group of males in the State's prison system to a critical mass in some facilities, and to constituting a majority in others. They spread so fast that everyone was caught off guard. Not only was the prison system changed, but the entire criminal landscape on the local neighborhood level in every city and small town where gang culture appeared. The boundary lines of loyalty were redrawn overnight. Prior to gangs it was respect,  infamy, crews, family ties, or how much money you made that earned you esteem in the neighborhood. After the gangs came on the scene male status began to be determined by gang status (rank), the size of your following, and taste for violence.  Those who were charismatic, clever, and violent ascend in the ranks.

Even so, I had the early suspicion these groups would not be successful as criminal enterprises. I did not see the discipline, dedication, and intelligence that was required to hold immature egos together in an organized crime syndicate. Gang culture took the existing Black criminal culture and froze it at the adolescent stage of development, where it remains  today. Most of these males were very young, ranging from 14-25, apart from a few in prison they were not reading books, studying military tactics, political science, philosophy or technology. It struck me as odd (and scary) that these gangs were not even clandestine movements trying to be secret about their aims. Their criminal intent was on full display.

# CRIMINALITY - THE OLD MODEL - VS- THE NEW MODEL

Although I was young (in my 20s) when the gang movement began to spread, their agenda was antithetical to my concept of criminality and its purpose. I grew up in an era (1980s & 1990s) where the shadow of the Italian Mafia was still felt. Their myth as loyal organized crime families took root in our corrupted imaginations. It was their model of criminals posing as businessmen that we aspired to emulate. We wanted to get to a level of refinement where nobody could tell who or what we were; our toughness was proven through our willingness to fight and shoot (individually or collectively), our ruthlessness was something carefully cultivated by experience and hidden from ordinary eyes. That means when you were in position you were no longer to act like a gangster, move like a gangster, talk like a gangster, or appear to be a gangster. If it was possible you were to transcend criminality altogether, but only remain true to the underworld code and the people in your heart. Gangsterism was always just a stepping stone to legitimacy. It was never to be criminality for the sake of criminality or for fame.

In the 1990s, to evade law enforcement surveillance, we were transitioning from being neighborhood posses, gangs, cliques, crews and sets, with wild names, to secret society style crews with regional or national reach and no names. We were abandoning names because groups with names could be easily identified and indicted. We wanted to have a tight knit group who were invisible, fluid, and anonymous to outsiders. Our actions and association were intentionally incognito and obscure. As Sun Tzu said: "be [adaptable and changeable ] like water". Your "set" was just the block you were from or the local gang that ran that area. Most drug "sets" were made up of multiple individuals, cliques, crews, and families in competition with each other.

Naming the "set" seemed mandatory in the 1980s, but naming crews was optional. Sometimes law enforcement would name you. Sets or crew names were usually based on the address or name of the street or the name of the housing project where the set was located. For example, here are fictional demonstrations: 47th street Boyz (or 47 Boyz), Maple Tree Housing Projects (MTP, MOB, or MTP Mafia), Douglas Street Boyz (D-Block Boyz or D-Boyz). Crews are most likely made up of people who grew up together and are acquainted by friendship or relatives. Your crew was whoever you did crime with, and those who participated in the scheme and ate at your table. Men and women were bound by mutual respect, secrets, responsibilities, and profits.

It was the criminal network and participation of members which defined who was part of the organization; it had nothing to do with initiations, announcing our membership, flag carrying, colors, outfits, or formal structure. The leader was whoever supplied the drugs and organized the money-making aspect of the network. Violence and fear had its place, but profit was the cement holding everything together. This method of organization continues to be used because it is the most efficient local arrangement, considering the circumstances. Nas summarize our aspirations:

A drug dealers dream,
stashed cream
keys on a triple beam
500 SL  green
95 nickel gleam
Condominium.....
Thug dressed like a gentleman...
Tailor made ostrich...
Chanel for my woman friend. 18

Nas

Whereas this new breed of criminal gang-members were broadcasting to the world their intentions. Whether it was their bright colors, flag carrying, loud talking, aggressiveness, moving in big groups, hand gestures, dread locks, or  tagging,  it all seemed like a step backward in the evolution of crime. They were acting like the Los Angeles street gangs of the 1970 & 80s in the pre-crack era, before accumulating wealth became the objective of Black gangsterism. These new bangers did not appear to want money, it appeared as though they just wanted to do bad things to weaker people and be recognized for being tough or crazy. Many simply wanted to be infamous.

I quickly discovered a prevalent trait among them was the pathological need to be recognized, and if you ignored them and their new credentials they got agitated. If you did not take the time to find out a gang banger's name or showed no interest in their ridiculous life they were peeved. I soon realized that many of them were needy males, who needed constant attention: *look at me I'm tough, look at me see how they fear me, see how they listen to me, I got this many niggas under me, so and so is my big homie.* There was definitely a certain type that was attracted to this movement. For my part, I simply never recognized any gang authority  or hierarchy, the rules of their world did not apply to me. If you got in my way I'm going to hurt you no matter if you're a five-star general or a pup, they were all the same in my eyes.  Many of my peers dismissed them as clowns, those who did embrace this movement were already veteran criminals who joined gangs only for a few reasons:

to exploit the structure and manipulate young males,

or they joined because they were afraid to be left behind this new popular wave;

or joined before they became victims of this violent energy;

or you joined a gang to become the opposition of a gang that had momentum in recruiting. (I don't know any male to join a gang to be a revolutionary).

If you see males committing acts of violence and instilling fear in the local population, but you don't want to be a follower or are resentful or scared,  the next thing for you to do is join the opposition gang or start an opposition gang. This is said to be the origins of the L. A. Bloods street gangs, who were banding together to resist the growing violence of the Crips. According to an article in the Source Magazine, one veteran gang member (Conceptione) speaking about the origins of the Bloods and Crips beef said (to paraphrase)  that: *the Crips was a bunch of dark-skinned dudes running around beating up light-skinned dudes and the Bloods formed to be their opposition.* The rise of the Crips in New York and New Jersey was a direct response to the absurd aggression of the Bloods. Some of my friends turned "Crip" just to spite the neighborhood Bloods. I would imagine such things occur in many places.

Fast forward, in my opinion, if you were a gangster over twenty when the gang wave hit in the 1990s and 2000s you only joined the gang to use the teenagers, who were the real believers swelling the ranks. This too conflicted with many of our beliefs, because we were not building criminal networks based off the idea of manipulation but trust, loyalty, and family. How can your crew be loyal if they think, assume, or realize that you don't care about them, and only want to use them? How can such a crew last? The answer is, it can't. This is why the gangs were/are always engaged in fratricide. There was an inside joke among my peers that the gang movement was made up of all the "rejects," the dudes who could not make it as hustlers in the game, or those who just wanted to be down with something.

The males that are successful drug dealers really have no incentive to join a gang other than to protect their enterprise from ambitions gang members looking for a reason to attack, or the drug dealer sees the gang's rise as inevitable and want to use the structure to improve his organization. When the gangs moved in, established drug dealers with their influence and violent reputation, were getting preferential treatment and rank. With their neighborhood influence they could turn an entire crew, block, or housing project into new members overnight. This is how the drug dealers got "status" in gangs without getting jumped in, 'drilling' or putting in "work". Whether it was the Bloods or Crips the allure of the gang movement was powerful, young males and females in the early 2000s were under tremendous pressure to conform to this new subculture, which was presented as  cool to be down with and dangerous to resist.

Gang structure did not eliminate the old secret society model of local organization, rather, it superimposed another organization overtop of the exiting one and forced the two to coexist. While the neighborhood crew is still the basic organizing unit of urban criminals, the new national gang structure took dozens of crews, cliques, and individual petty criminals from different parts of the city, different towns, and States and made them part of a gang franchise. Where the highest ranks of gang status is strictly controlled by a central body, who may be located in a different state.

Although there is constant turnover at the top of the gang hierarchy because of indictments and death, for the most part these are stable structures that immediately replace dead or imprisoned leaders with new males. There are individuals (males and female), crews, projects, and sections of cities scattered nationwide who are now under the brand of the same gang. In fact, one large or small city is typically host to many gang franchises; this extends down to the neighborhood level which (depending where you are) can have gang members under different sets working together in the same crew. It is not unusual to have family members (even siblings) who belong to different sets. Under this new structure people who would not otherwise know or associate with each other, are now loosely affiliated under the same set and flag. Males from a small town in New Jersey can travel down to a small town in South Carolina and find members of his set.

This is a tribal/clan system of organization where the gang is the tribe, and the sets are the clans. The gang is a tribe that has removed the requirement that members be related by blood and custom, practically everything else of the structure has been left intact. Including the tradition where warriors, or violent males, are the strength and backbone of the group. There are very few elders in this system, patriarchs are dead or imprisoned, OGs and matriarchs have never existed. Where gang culture did radically alter criminal culture was in its leadership model. In my opinion, the first flaw of the new gang structure was how it gave status to violent males. No longer did intelligent males who knew how to organize a crew and drug set represent the primary movers of the underworld. It was chiefly violent males who rose in gang ranks and called the shots. This poses a problem because in the "hood" violent males are (intelligence aside), generally speaking, the most emotionally unstable, drug addicted, sociopathic, and amoral.

Linking status with violence gave them an incentive to be violent. If they wanted to move up in rank they did not have to put a scheme to generate revenue for the economic development of the gang. Rather, they had to act crazy and kill as many people, for the pettiest reasons possible. Usually under the excuse of expanding the gang territory or representing the set. In this context, the male is not seen as out-of -control if what he is doing (in his mind and in their eyes) is for "the set." Additionally, you are not going to settle disputes or "beef" if you have no interest to do so.

If it is beneficial for you to earn stripes by combat, then combat under any excuse will be the modus operandi. The same logic applies to ordering hits, if there is a social incentive to be gained by having people killed, then having people killed for almost nothing will be the way you operate. Young intelligent males are likely to be used, manipulated, or forced to engage in criminal activity that is outside their comfort zone. Young males, eager to prove themselves, are sent on "dummy missions" to destroy human life without any comprehension for the  damage he is about to inflict on this generation and the next.

Under the influence of a gang, adolescent males and females can go from being a naive aimless teenager into amoral predators in a matter of months. The gang's socialization process is completed by rituals like getting jumped in, tattooing,  and branding letters or symbols into the skin. Music, drugs, and criminal activity are also used to accelerate the corruption of the teen's moral fiber. It was explained to me that in order for the new gang member to go out and kill, he must first come to view his enemies as nothing, not even human.

It must be stressed that gang violence is different from common gangster "beef" with people you may know. The gangbanger who is killing has to sometimes target people that he doesn't even know for very vague and ill defined reasons. Not over money  or not disrespect, but just because they are who they are. Once the male or female becomes engaged in violence they are caught in a negative feedback loop, where the cycle of violence is perpetuated because he is both predator and prey or the hunted and the hunter, who exist in a state of permanent offense and defense.

It was strange to my peers that males with "status" were coming into neighborhoods (they were not from) claiming to have authority because the gang's franchise extended into that territory. This was an affront and offensive to my peers who would hear about gangs having people murdered (by young nobodies, fresh off the porch) in neighborhoods they didn't come from or control.  The males bringing these guys around were seen as traitors to their neighborhood. Welcoming criminals from rival towns (all other towns are considered rivals) to your neighborhood to call shots was the highest betrayal of the old order.

Since gang status is not determined by business acumen, but the ability to project fear, a dimwitted and broke male, who is feared, is likely to rise in the ranks faster than an intelligent male who knows how to make money and organize, but does not have an imposing presence. Ambitious young men who are very intelligent are overlooked in favor of males who are masters at swagger; hence, addiction, megalomania, insecurity, and stunning ignorance are common features of gang leadership and foot soldiers, and conflict is used to settle disputes.

This contributes to gang disorganization and the reason their structure is primitive. This increases the likelihood that a cycle of distrust continues and cooperation is difficult. Since addiction, early death, and long imprisonment are common features among the criminal class there are few middle aged gang members with enough credibility, power, or wisdom to control undisciplined young males. Adolescent males or adult males stuck at the adolescent stage of emotional development, make up the rank-and-file members and guide its evolution for better or worse. These testosterone-filled males with fragile egos make decisions based on instinct and whim. At most, they are thinking one step ahead at any moment.

Complex forms of organization cannot take shape in this environment. There is no organization with complex administration that has been created in the last 5,000 years that has not used intelligence as a test for advancing its members in rank. Religious organizations move layman and clerics up based on their knowledge of theology and ecclesiastic law. Schools/ Universities use academic performance and degrees to determine status of students, teachers professors, and scholars. Military personnel move up in rank based on their ability to follow orders well, displays of disciplined or academic accomplishment (those with college degrees move up in rank faster) the propensity for violence has nothing to do with rank; it is the generals who have West Point degrees in military strategy or logistics that give marching orders to the violent males in the infantry units. Law enforcement (local police, FBI, ATF DEA etc), attain rank based on aptitude and performance.

In sum, every organization that intends to be successful rewards men and women who are educated, disciplined, and perform their duties well. Being out-of-control is rewarded nowhere accept among the lowest levels of gang culture. Even so, gang culture is different everywhere you go, some places have much more sophisticated structure both within and outside the prison system. I would imagine older gangs with decades of experience have ironed out problems through natural evolution. Another factor determining the evolution or maturity of gangs is its economic condition. Gangs or organizations who are present in very important and lucrative geographic locations (black market corridors) are forced to develop the discipline, structure, hierarchy, and violence necessary to keep and manage their illicit trade. America's Black gangs are neither poverty stricken as gangs in third world countries nor do they have monopolistic control over any important sector of the economy, hence, they are not as funded, ruthless, or organized as the Latino gangs with foreign origins or cartel ties.

Looking over the prison population that I can observe, the low aptitude of the gang leadership is obvious. Most males are locked up for petty crimes or crimes of desperation. They often lack the support one would expect from being a member of a national organization with hundreds of members. This is a point that veteran criminals cannot wrap their minds around. I have heard it a million times: *"How is it that its so many of them but they can't do anything with their numbers?"* or *"Man if I had fifty or a hundred niggahs under me I would be unstoppable."* Some gang leaders have two hundred males, theoretically, under their command, yet end up in prison for low level crimes; and their mothers, sisters, girlfriends, become their primary support system. Being in a maximum security prison for two decades means I have seen the leaders of many gangs in an intimate setting. I can say without hesitancy that most of the males I observed are of average intelligence as far as mental faculties are concerned; they have good memories and reasonable deductive reasoning- their software works.

However, I believe they are far below average - vis a vis- the people they are up against, their real opposition. That is to say, law enforcement, other criminal organization, or males organized for violent confrontation, and economic exploitation. In truth the Black males I observe only excel at creating chaos and disorder, breaking things is their specialty, putting things together is their Achilles heel. The anti-intellectualism found among the urban poor is thoroughly present within this culture. The males I observe lack in depth understanding of basic concepts and have poor academic habits. One reasonably disciplined male with basic motor skills and ambition can stand in as a substitute for twenty of these males; and I say this as a general statement about the Black males I observe, not simply gang leaders.

***

That said, if gangs have anything positive they have an organic self-made structure for Black males to organize around. They have an entire system for verifying who is a member of what gang and particular set, and if his "line" (particular crew in a set) is "official." Lines can have dozens or hundreds of members. They regulate these sets and lines with constant communication (gossip) about who is no longer "official" (because of loss of status). Not only do they have ways of determining a member's actual rank or status in their organizations, but where, when, and who it came from. They also have ways to strip undeserving males of position. The status of an individual or group is usually lost when a leader of a line or an individual within the line turns (is discovered as) informant, or if one line has lost a conflict with another set. They even have ways of folding the remaining good (solid) members of one set or line into another set after the line is "dead" (because the leader of the line has lost status by becoming an informant).

153

When New Jersey gangs began they had rituals and quasi-religious components in their organization like burning paws into their arms, fasting requirements, and rules against homo-sexuality. When I heard young gang members discussing "fasting" I was impressed with this aspect, because at the time I was studying literature on Islamic mysticism and knew the power in such practices. But I have not heard of fasting taking root in the organization as a common practice. If a gang can be described as criminal religion then the "set" would be analogous to a religious sect; each set has its own rules in matters of who qualifies to be a member. This also includes the basic structure of its hierarchy and ranking system. Some gangs allow females, while some allow all races, etc.

Like religious sectarian strife, there are schisms where groups split from old sets and form new ones with their own rules and regulations - this process is never ending. That said, I see very stable gang structures which use the historic status of the gang or set to maintain legitimacy. Breakaway sets are considered illegitimate or "not official" and their members are "green lighted" for attack. This ensures that few test the bounds of the gangs authority. I am told that New York/ New Jersey (among others) Blood sets are not considered official sets when you enter the federal prison system. But, in truth, "official" simply means those who have enough members and the violence to defend themselves from critics.

***

When Black gangs appeared within the prison system they caught everybody's attention, but Muslims and Latino gangs dominated them numerically and had little to fear, so they were at first dismissed as irrelevant. These young males were not (and never have been) organized enough to monopolize the drug trade or any other black market, so they could not stand in the way of other groups making money. If anything they were dependent on the old networks and had to conform to the existing power structures.

Prison administrations also made the mistake of forcing gang members together in order to isolate them (in "Gang units") this only strengthened the gang structure and made them appear more dangerous. According to one high ranking member, when the New York prison system and the federal government began sending gang members out of New York because of their violent activity, the exiled members began "breeding" in whatever state county jails they were sent. This government policy, he says, was the primary reason for the gang's initial proliferation throughout New Jersey and the country.

Like other groups they began to use the cover of religious services to meet and communicate, few were sincere in their worship. At first they were discouraged from attending church and were not allowed to pray or attend Jumu'ah services because rank-and-file Muslims were hostile to this new element. But gang members were very bellicose, persistent, and kept growing. Those who came from Muslim backgrounds were indignant about not being welcomed in Islamic prayers or services. I can recall in 2002 that Muslims were being asked to help run the Bloods out of the Church services in Garden State Youth Correctional facility (GSYCF) because they were loud and disruptive. By 2003 corrections officers, who had always feared Muslims in the prison system, were saying: "I'm not scared of Muslims, I'm scared of the Bloods."

Fast forward to 2022, current and former gang bangers now make up significant portions of the Islamic community and Christian leadership in prison. They have not only penetrated the Islamic ranks and services in full force, but, in my opinion, now constitute the majority of some prison communities. Make no mistake about it, former and current Bloods and Crips are the leaders of the church and dominate the Muslim ranks. Some of them are just as sincere in their study and devotion than non gang-affiliated believers.

In some cases their narrow-minded tribal/ warrior mentality helps them excel within religious ranks. Those gifted with charisma continue to be influential when they enter religious communities. New Jersey has a very limited diversity of gangs, unlike other states, so I suspect that wherever there are a variety of gangs that the culture is different in some cases and much the same in other ways. It is amusing to listen to Friday sermons where the Imam is castigating gang banging, yet 80 percent of the males under 40 in the audience are active gang members. Some of the most zealous Muslims and Christians are those who have come out of the gang movement.

Before the advent of gangs geographic origin and ethnicity was the primary factor in determining a person's place upon entering prison. The male would enter prison and be directed to those from his city or those of his ethnic tribe, where he would quickly discover who the alpha males and OGs were and why they had risen to such status -which was probably through a combination of violence, intelligence, charisma, experience and longevity. They are survivors who have made it through the crucible of street life and prison and maintained their sanity, dignity and respect. If the new male was not already known, older prisoners would interrogate him about his credentials, which include: what section of the city he was from, what neighborhood he claimed, his drug set/ crew affiliations, and family tree. All of which proved his origins and whether he was a bona fide criminal.

His credentials would be cross-checked by phone calls and questioning of his peers and those from his neighborhood. If he checked out, his place in the hierarchy was determined by age, intelligence, aggression, criminal maturity, street status, economic status, and ambition. If he had a suspect background and his origins were questionable, that is, if nobody knew him, he had no crew or known family, then he was allowed around but kept at a distance. If it was discovered that he had cooperated with law enforcement any time (his fate was determined by what prison he was in or if he was in a federal or state system) he would be kept around but never fully embraced, but males from other towns were not informed about his suspect status, except on a need-to-know basis.

Older males would guide younger males according to their values and his potential, and he would be given the necessary items required for him to get comfortable: clothes, sneakers, televisions, and food. If he asked for books they would be given to  him. If he was part of a religious community he was informed of the ropes and the politics. If he wanted to sell drugs they would walk him through this process (of measuring quantities for maximum profits) and give him the ins and outs of the facility, its markets, and its clientele. If he was a drug addict  he would be warned about that path, but accommodated without taking advantage of him.

If he had something to bring to the table then his value would be determined in terms of what he could contribute to the criminal enterprise (that is the everyday prison existence). He would have support should he have problems with males from other towns, and disputes between towns were settled by the alpha males  talking it out before things got out of hand. Young males would also be introduced to everyone who could possibly make his time easier, whether it was the paralegal with their knowledge, or those who controlled the black market prison goods.

Prior to gangs the internal transformation of  a person was a personal affair.  If he no longer believed in the values of his past criminal life he could denounce them to himself and distance himself from the males who were not on his path. He could remain alone, or join any group he thought would lead him to salvation - whatever that looked liked to him. However, today when a person leaves the gang and his heart is no longer in it,  he is,  nevertheless, connected to the politics of the gang. Males resentful of his departure and change of heart will hold this against him, and the enemies he made while banging will not care about his change of heart  or new-found religion. In fact, the reason he left in the first place will become the subject of debate. E.g. whether he left because of honest change of heart or because his secrets (like informing in a past case) are catching up to him and he wants the protection of another organization. This makes the gang member's conversion to religion even more suspect. Now even honest self-transformation of the individual is looked at suspiciously, called into question, and held against him. Even after leaving the gang the ex-member must remain emotionally on defense and hyper vigilant.

Now that gangs politics are the norm, young males come to prison and are either directed to the guys from his town or those who belong to his particular  set - who could be from anywhere. Most likely they are not going to be mature males who can guide him in the right direction or offer him a new perspective of the world. More like young males who will reinforce his existing beliefs and behavior, further his corruption for their gain, and push him into the prison culture of gang politics before he gets a chance to figure out who to trust or what direction he wants to go.  If he has resources they will be used by gang members to get high or hustle until they are depleted. The situation is complicated if three new males from the same town enter prison, and they all belong to different gangs or different sets of the same gang - those sets might even be at war with  each.

Under these conditions, older males have to back away from guiding younger males because the loyalties of the latter are always suspect. Not only is there an age gap, but a cultural one as well. Mature males now have little hand in guiding young males who orbit their space, but never come into their sphere of influence.  Violence is the elephant in the room of every conversation and interaction in prison. When you have males whose loyalty is in question it breaks down all semblance of trust and cooperation. It is not that  gang culture destroyed the old arrangement entirely, but the old system has now been undermined although it was  durable and organic..

****

Again, the problem with the gang structure is not the actual structure, but the personnel. These organizations are populated by drug addicted males, who do not take the accumulation of knowledge or education seriously. The intellectual life of the gang banger is dismal, they have no standard curriculum and are not required to memorize any knowledge of substance. Other than knowing their gang's personal history, laws, slang, or codes they have no literary tradition. The entire scope of required study could cover a few pages at most.

Most gang members I know are consumed by social media, rap culture, pop culture, and sports. These are the sources of their philosophical, spiritual, and moral training. In general, their moral compass is driven by survival instincts, drug abuse, and pathological materialism; most of the violent crime being committed is driven by petty beefs and the desire to wear Gucci and other designer apparel. There is no truth except the truth that gets them what they want, they are unapologetically amoral. The gangster code, which they claim to live by, holds no weight in the minds of most. Ambition, manipulation and distrust are the underpinnings to that life. Gang members associated with religious groups may fare a little better because they have a moral code to reference.

Gang culture always begins as an arms race for numbers (recruitment). The gangs desperately  want to get their numbers up so they settle for quantity instead of quality; accepting such low breed characters exposes these organizations to elevated risks. This is why snitching has risen to be such a topic of concern in the hood. Even though these are well known transnational gangs they are not composed of soldiers bound by an oath and the code of Omerta. Many of these young males are unprepared intellectually and emotionally when confronted by state and federal authorities, who dangle a life or death sentence over their heads. One weak link (let alone many) can dismantle an entire organization and give RICO indictments to everybody. Law enforcement are in the habit of charging petty gang members with racketeering as if they were organized criminal syndicates.

As a consequence, these groups are infiltrated with informants at every level. Snitching is so prevalent  to gang culture that exposing those who have "told before" or is an active informant is a taboo subject. Males are no longer weeded out and subject to attack, on the contrary, they are shielded from criticism if they are a high ranking member  with legions of followers, or the family of someone with status. It is not uncommon for someone to be punished or killed for exposing an informant.  As a paralegal I have been privy to the legal cases of gang members and the gossip; as such I can say with confidence there are very few leaders who are not, at some point in time, suspected of being  informants.

All in all, an untold sum of Black genius and Black life is wasted due to street life and gangsterism. What it costs our community is readily apparent when it is realized what  young males and females are able to accomplish, when their energies  are directed to areas other than the politics of gang power. When these males focus their study on law, religion, music, writing or academic pursuits they are able to achieve the most impressive feats - in a very short time. Like memorization of entire books, proficiency in law, competency in skills, and trades. I have met the most intelligent males who are masters at all sorts of hustles, arts, and disciplines. There is nothing wrong with the deductive reasoning or motor skills of most males in prison. I object to those who paint the picture that the prison population is made up of special needs prisoners. If they are intelligent and you speak to them intelligently they will reciprocate.

Most of the gang bangers I have met wish they never joined a gang, they are mature enough to know that they were used as pawns in some fools (or their own) criminal fantasy. They wish to leave it, but feel compelled to keep flying their flag out of peer pressure and the feeling that it is too late and complicated to back out. The gang banger who wants to "drop his flag" is essentially denouncing allegiance to all his friends and social network. Gang members have to be extremely brave to do this. Those who break away (without violent repercussion) from the gang and its politics are disliked by all current members who look at former members like they were never with the movement in the first place.

I can say with certainty that a gang member is more likely to be killed, betrayed, set up, robbed, assaulted, hurt by a member of their own gang than an opposition gang. All the beef,  hate, jealousy, jockeying for status, power and position that results in murder is usually the result of intra-group rivalry. In prison 95 percent of gang fights and stabbings happen between members of the same gang. The people that are quickest to use you, humiliate you, turn you in, rat on you,  and take what you have are your own gang. Period. Crips don't have to worry about Bloods more than they have to worry about Crips. Vis Versa. Think about it, all these legendary gang leaders that are celebrated are most likely the victim of their own set or different set and not a rival gang. Young members must think deep before they join a gang because they may have just become friends with their future killers.

It is not surprising that many gang members find it difficult to drop their flags and renounce their gang ties. When males have invested years into sacrificing their bodies for the set, suffering for the set, and representing the set - by fighting, killing, and putting in work -  their entire identities are tied to their position within these movements. When we approach these males about changing their lives and abandoning their beliefs we must understand what they are holding on to and what they are being asked to give up. We are asking them to  reject their tribe and commit social suicide.

************************

As a general rule, males are violent creatures.  If he is in a poverty stricken environment he will organize his cohorts into a wolf pack and rob, kill, and steal in this fashion, whether they have a name or not. Those males with means, who have a desire to destroy things and people, will often kill outside of his environment in a much more orderly fashion; whether as a lone wolf,  military, or paramilitary (public or civic) organization. The gang is seen as particularly dangerous because dozens, hundreds, or thousands  move as a single predatory organism. The real intractable problem with the national gang structure is  it institutionalizes violence, spectacle, and ritual. There is simply no gang without violence. It subsumes the personal identity of the individual, and makes it difficult for the individual to break free of its psychological and emotion grip. To deny the gang is to deny yourself.

I have sat around not only "former" gangbangers but men in their sixties who have not  banged in forty years, nevertheless, when they reminisce about the gang's beginning and how they rose in rank, they are transported back in time. When they reminisce about wars and fights, you perceive they are not talking about the past (what they used to do or who they used to be), they are in the present - still in the gang  - just removed from the action or the politics. Their body and mind are detached from the organization but their hearts long for a movement that was once great. This is even true for local neighborhood gangs or crews, who don't have the national or regional presence of well-known organizations. However, it is much easier to break away and distance yourself from neighborhood gangs, because it is only your local identity that is being transcended.

There is a common misconception that must be cleared up. The presence of gangs in a poverty stricken neighborhood does not necessarily make the neighborhood more dangerous or violent than poverty stricken neighborhoods without them. What is true is that when a gang is establishing itself in a new territory violence escalates. This has many causes including: an ascendant gang inflicting violence on the population to make them submit to the gangs new order;   the formation of gang factions who are warring with each other;   those resisting the new movement forming their own distinct gangs,  who are also creating their own factions who are also in conflict.

All of these scenarios lead to the spike in neighborhood violence. It is one thing for such a phenomenon  to happen where there is historically low crime, it is quite another for this to happen where there is historically high crime. Gangs sometimes take years and decades to resolve internal strife, but once the dust is settled and internal differences are ironed out through violence, they are usually able to manage internal violence much better. This process may take years, until one gang assumes supremacy over a space, and the gang culture becomes normalized.

When this happens gang identity is simply incidental to the perpetrator's crime. This phenomenon   is also true in prison. I have been in a maximum security prison over two decades and it is far less violent now (with four different gangs and eight different sets) then it was twenty years ago (with two gangs). Even when it is violent the violence is not generally gang related. Cities like New York, Newark, and Camden etc, are proof of this concept. They were all much more violent in the 1990s, when there were only local neighborhood crews. Now that they are saturated with multiple national gangs, they have much lower murder rates than they did three decades ago. That said according to the FBI statistics as of 2022 violence nation wide is up 30% in the last three years, but there is no way to attribute this to the rise in gang culture. Instead it is  part of a larger trend where guns have completely saturated America, law enforcement has strategically (vindictively)  retreated from policing,  and criminality has become a way of life.

I think once the gang culture is able to 'mature', the presence of the gang organization prevents there being an free-for-all, or a culture of war of "all against all." When gangs focus on getting money they have the mechanisms in place to resolve internal conflicts for the "greater good." Nevertheless, violence is enshrined into gang activity as law and cities do not fair well when gangs are introduced to them, this culture can  permanently alter the nature of criminality for the worst.

I do not avoid  my past statements about gangsterism and gangs. I think this class is very dangerous and must be held in check by any means necessary, if we want our communities to  thrive. No man, woman, or child can prosper in an environment governed by adolescent males with machines guns and god complexes. And businesses cannot prosper in an atmosphere where there is no predictable order.  It is the primary interest of Black people that the rise of gangsterism and gang culture be constantly monitored and held in check. We must push back against these black holes, which are sucking our children into them. We cannot be afraid to confront the reality of what these organizations are, and what they are doing to generations of young people. If a gang movement is introduced into an area and it is possible to destroy the organization in its infancy, steps should be taken to wipe it out with ALL necessary ruthlessness; no expense should be spared in trying to save a neighborhood from this cancer. When confronting violent males and criminal fraternities, attacking the problem sooner than later is the best policy. The aim is to prevent the gang culture from becoming deeply rooted in the environment. The longer these groups are allowed to thrive the more emboldened they become, and invincible they look; this is what makes them alluring to younger generations. Purging this element must be done with precision, the first generations of leaders and recruiters have to be dealt with extreme cruelty, as well as, the first generation of young disciples. By 'ruthlessness and cruelty' I mean to suggest that extra-judicial actions cannot be ruled out- all options must be on the table in this type of situation. The question for us is how much gang activity and gangsterism is too much?

That said, I do not believe that gangs can be destroyed. They are durable institutions that change and take on new shapes whenever they are under pressure. That means they are probably a permanent part of the urban landscape for the foreseeable future, and instead of acting like they don't exist, we have to find a better way to integrate them into our systems. The organic structures (local, regional, and national) they have created for themselves can be utilized in creative ways, it is better to take a system they already understand and use it rather than trying to impose something on them from the top down - which they are bound to resist.

In any case, gangs are a symptom of a larger problem. Particularly, generational poverty, desperation, the breakdown of strong family households and communities headed by responsible men and women. These males are drawn from the same exact fatherless/manless homes that gave birth to our criminal culture. At the end of the day, we know who they are and what they need. We cannot allow ourselves to be scared away from them by the dark personas they have taken on to cover up their fear, shame, and ignorance. The bottom line is this, a significant portion of our warrior aged males are finding their fraternal camaraderie and security in their local gang sets, and  if we want to save them we have to approach them in all seriousness.

I have witnessed gang activity up close for over two decades, and I do not believe that these males are incorrigible or hopeless cases. These young males and females show tremendous loyalty and dedication to their gangs; they cry and feel pain at the loss of their friends, they sacrifice and accept suffering for the greater "good" of the set when they must. Their moral compass is flawed, but their mental faculties themselves are sound and only misdirected. Many of them will accept right guidance and conform to superior organization when it is presented to them in a no nonsense manner. They are no different than men and women who want to be led, fed, and guided by leaders who are not hypocrites. The most problematic aspect of  our venture with this element is that, in addition to being undisciplined and drug addicted, many of them are compromised with respect to their cooperation with law enforcement; their ranks are saturated with informants. This is not simply a problem for criminal organizations but any group that demands the trust in its members. Apart from this, I believe our primary obstacle is working to realign the moral compass of  misguided  males and females.

# THE "DEMONS"

## THE BLACK MALE 'S  WORSHIP OF VIOLENCE

There is another dangerous aspect of this culture that we must address if we are to deal with these males - and increasingly females. If we are going to guide these young people,  out of the darkness that is their minds, we must be sober and approach this subject with an iron will. I am speaking about the worship of violence that has become fashionable as of late. We are in a time of degeneracy, where murder has become like blood sport to urban males. I am even reluctant to reveal these psychological traits that appear to be prevalent among the urban criminal subclass;  but I believe we do more harm trying to hide the truth rather than confronting  it head on.

In 2021, a woman in Philadelphia was purportedly raped in a subway terminal while on lookers watched and nobody stepped in to intervene. Instead, some recorded the episode on their phones. It had nothing to do with gangs, but nonetheless, it was an apathetic mentality that I had observed by watching and listening to gang bangers for decades. This was shocking to most but it was only disappointing to me. It was a state of mind that I had been observing for a period of time. I had been taking note that young males, in particular, make it a point to let others know how much they don't care about anything or any body. Being heartless, emotionless, and unsympathetic is not a novel philosophical posture among the urban criminal, but there is something new in the way that such thoughts are expressed.

Some years ago, I began to observe that males not only began to brag about the number of their killings to strangers, but that they talked about murder and killing with a sort of giddiness. I do not deny that males of my generation spoke about such topics, but, as a rule, this is not a line of dialogue that I recall being a cultural norm. I have consulted others on this point and they concur with my assessment. Conversely, males of my era went out of their way to avoid conversations about their past deeds; because you did not want that information to come back and bite you. Quite often, if the subject of a crime was to arise, the listener would warn the speaker *"Yo don't tell me about that,"* or indicate that they were not interested in hearing something that could hurt you. But murder is no longer a taboo subject, on the contrary, it is treated as a badge of honor.

Being from a violent city like Camden NJ, I know hundreds of people who have been killed; some were friends others just acquaintances. But death, no matter who it was and the circumstances, was always a sobering reality. It always brought reflection to mind and made us think about the fragility of our existence. When everybody around you dies young you cannot help but wonder *'am I next or what if that was me'*. When we heard of a new death it was a somber moment of reflection. Unless the person was a pure menace to society, his death was not laughed at or cheered. If anything, we took a second to think about what the death meant and moved on. Death did not induce laughter among my peers, someone might say "fuck that niggah," but laughter, giggling, and joking was not a common affect. I cannot say the same is true anymore.

I meet young males who barley know me, but find the need to let me know they got "five bodies" to their credit, or they "give all dome (head) shots" or they 'don't miss.' They think they are going to impress someone and make them look like real men or gangster, but it doesn't, it makes them look like evil little kids. They believe they should be respected for their predatory achievements, and the highest praise should be given to them for what they accomplished. But I don't see that, I see young men who are so empty and starved for attention that they will destroy your life and theirs, just to be recognized and respected. Again, I do not try to idealize the past, males of my generation did things for recognition. The rap group Gang Starr raised this very issue in the track: "*Just to get a rep*" (1991) which was an early criticism of this type of warped psychology. Nas also criticized this attention seeking behavior when he said: "*It's like the game ain't the same, got younger niggaz pullin triggers bringing fame to they name....*" *N.Y. state of Mind* (1994).

However, this destructive psychology is so epidemic and prevalent that it could be classed as a new norm, where adolescent males are pathologically obsessed with being a gangster and killing for recognition. I believe this mindset, which was already present in both the larger American culture and the urban subculture, was exacerbated by the gang movement - and has been able to infect the entire culture through the music. The gang member, not the lone gangster, is the now the model criminal for those considering a path of violence. For the last 20 years being seen as gang affiliated or acknowledged as being a murderer has become a prime objective of too many urban males. Killing has now taken on the air of entertainment, comedic revelry, and blood sport; where killers taunt the victim's families and the victims after they are dead, as a way to both take credit for the crime, and rub it in their face that he got away with it. Advances in social media technology coupled with gang culture has created a cultural cesspool of taunting and killing, and killing and taunting.

When the song "*Who shot Yah*" from NOTORIOUS B.I.G. came out (1995), it was a shock to the urban hip hop culture. I remember sitting back and thinking '*yo this shit is crazy, these niggaz is braggin about hittin Tupac and clowning him, these niggaz is on some different, dark shit, with this song.*' That is how out-of-the-ordinary such behavior was. Everybody assumed that it was a taunt to Tupac who had just gotten shot in New York, and was blaming B.I.G. for setting him up. B.I.G. said the song was made a long time before Tupac got shot, but nonetheless, he had to understand the effect such a track would have at that moment. When Tupac made *"hit' em up"*, (1996) and went after New York rappers it was a departure from the norm, because it was explicit in taunting and threatening violence against specifically named artist - over the radio or "on wax." Hit' em up is actually called the "best diss track ever," but I don't consider it a simple diss track. Only because it crossed the bounds of being deadly serious.

Make no mistake about it, rap music has had violent lyrics for a very long time, but up until a national figure like Tupac Shakur and the Death Row Records camp (an openly gang affiliated organization) began to personalize their violent lyrics, nobody was talking about real conflict on wax. Most so-called "diss" tracks of the 1980s and 90s were just that, diss tracks. Diss tracks were not violent rants against particular people - that threatened bodily harm - by someone who is known to affiliate with gang members. Tupac was known to be an intense person, for those who were paying attention to the culture, it did not seem that he could back down from where he had taken it. I cannot say for certain that Tupac invented this kind of violent beef on wax, because hip hop subculture is so diverse there is no way to say that it had never been done.

However, there was never a nationally recognized figure who had taken the music in this direction. Even today when people see young males out of control and trying to prove himself to everyone, they say he "thinks he's Tupac." Or, "he's going through his Tupac stage." While others readily admit that they are channeling Tupac's energy. As much as he is celebrated by the culture, rarely does anyone comment on the destructive energy that Tupac released into Hip hop. His militancy and political consciousness is there for those who want to be inspired, but his false gangster persona exerts just as powerful an influence over the culture. Good or bad, people get from Tupac what they want and none of them are wrong in what they see.

For their part, East coast rappers were not use to this level of violent escalation in the music. If anyone paid attention, they would realize that NY artist were so shocked by 'Hit'em up' that most of them did not respond when called out, Jay–Z & Nas in particular. Mobb Deep was the only group called out that gave a direct response, they were already veterans of violent rap. Prior to this personalized attack in "Hit' em up," violent rappers spoke in generalities about killing and robbing people, or about his stressed state of mind. The gangsta rapper talked about common scenarios experience by inner-city males or invented fictitious accounts of violent episodes.

It was generally understood that the rapper had once been a criminal or criminal adjacent, and so understood the inner workings and psychology of this class. And this knowledge gave him the authority to speak on these subjects. Furthermore, the fury of violent rappers from the 1980s & 1990s was, for the most part, directed at the government or the system; some rappers were talking about conflict with other people, while others were voicing their anger over society's injustice. He was cursing the system and jousting with invisible enemies, and articulating rage through verse. When they talked about drug dealing, murder, and carjacking they were expressing that society had driven them to such behavior; they were not necessarily bragging about their behavior, but lamenting their fallen state. The rappers of the 1980s & 1990s were not proud of their criminal mindedness, they knew the urban family was in a degenerate condition. It was understood the artist was speaking for the criminal or poverty stricken class, and articulating urban mental and economic suffering. As violent and troubled as DMX was, he was clearly suffering and being haunted in his music. These were elegies of pain, remorse, and tragedy.

The so called 'gangster rappers' of today cannot act like they were once criminals, they have to actively *be* criminals or they have no credibility. If a rapper is talking about the gangster life he must now move beyond mere words. And demonstrate to his fans that he is, not only a certified criminal, but an active gang member. Furthermore, , there is an entire genre of rap whose subject matter focuses on bragging about hunting, shooting, and killing "the opposition" (opps). This is not a subculture of rap, but mainstream music and artist. A rapper can now talk about 'drilling' (hunting &

killing) with absolute seriousness and then do a Burger King or Sprite advertisement, and not look like a sellout. Rappers of the 1990s could not have navigated these two worlds, without looking like they 'sold out' (their street credentials) to the industry. Gang members of today have found a way to commercialize their culture, and operate both in the corporate world of hip hop - while maintaining ties to the underworld of gang life and violent conflict. Nas commented on this growing trend in rap in 2004, when he described the real violent beef between rap camps and rich rap artist as "Star Wars." Nas also characterized the rap industry itself as "organized crime."

There are so many shootings and murders behind this music (between gangs and rap camps)  that Black people in the industry are, for the first time, admitting that "rap music is dangerous," and has been affecting generations in negative ways. Such conversations were forbidden just a few years ago, nobody in the industry would have admitted that rap was harmful to the culture. Now, even major concert promoters like Live Nation are threatening not to book certain artist who make "diss"  tracks, and radio DJs are saying that they will not play certain "drill" music. What conscious rap artist and Black leaders have been saying for over three decades is finally being taken seriously, because the connection between rap's ideology and urban psychology cannot be denied. The only music genres surrounded by a specter of violence and commercial profit comparable to rap are Dance Hall reggae and Narco Corridos coming out of Mexico, which are often ballads celebrating cartel figures. All these subcultures are obsessed with  gangsterism and the commercialization of violence through song. However, rap outstrips these other genres in terms of its global reach and influence.

*...all the motherfuckin hustlas and drug dealers now want to be rappers.. and all of the fake rappers... want to be hustlas and drug dealers, but don't know how deep the game is...What part of the game is this?*

Last Dayz

ONYX (1996) 19

What ONYX observed all those years ago is now fully embodied in the rap culture. During the writing of this section the hip hop industry has been shaken up by notable events. In May 2022 Atlanta rappers Young Thug and Gunna, along with 26 others, were arrested and indicted for a slew of charges. Among the charges were racketeering, drug trafficking, car jacking, robbery, and murder. The crimes cover a decade of activity. It is alleged that Young Thug's YSL (Young Stoner Life) label was actually a criminal street gang. Young Thug is said to belong to the Sex Money Murder Blood set, and Gunna (who is actually a kid from the suburbs) belongs to a Crip set.

I was prompted to research how many other rappers were in legal trouble during the writing of this section. I found out there was a list of over 20 rappers who were currently locked up or facing years in prison related to gang violence, murder, and drug dealing. I believe all these males are gang members. These are very influential artist, many are multi-millionaires. Young Thug, being the most internationally known, was featured in Vogue magazine, where he modeled couture dresses.

Casanova – RICO - Drug distribution/ Alleged to be a leader in the Untouchable Gorilla Stone Nation Bloods.

Young Thug –RICO 56 count indictment

Gunna – RICO- 56 count indictment

42 Dugg- Gang activity- warrant / Arrested on private Jet

OJ Da Juiceman - unregistered Handgun

ASAP Rocky – Linked to a shooting- Arrested getting off a Private Jet

Rod Wave

Bankroll Freddie – Firearms/ Drug possession

Pooh Shiesty - 63 months for a shootout

Hoodrich Pablo Juan- RICO

9lokkNine- Firearms possession

Rio Da Yung OG- Drug trafficking

YFN Lucci – RICO Gang activity

Tay K - Convicted of multiple murders doing 55 years

Ar Ab  doing 50 year sentence for drug operation

03 Greedo

Foogiano - fugitive

YNW Melly Two counts of first degree murder

Kay Flook - First degree murder

Ralo – Drugs

Favio Foreign - shooting

DDG - Handgun


This list is not complete, but only represents "notable" artist. Females are not exempt from this infamy list.  They are also seduced by the culture and succumbing to criminal mindedness; they are just as gang affiliated,  and promoters of the criminal lifestyle, as their male peers. When *'rappers who have been shot'* is entered into a search engine, it generates an entirely new list. And when *'rappers who have been murdered'* is entered into a search, the result is a list of almost a hundred dead males, who have been shot to death, 20 rappers have been killed from January to May just in 2022. This is further evidence that music is not simply 'entertainment,' but a full-fledge ideology and lifestyle. People cannot listen to music and go unaffected by the nihilistic message.

Much of this ground was covered in my first book *Reflection of the Son in the section: Rap /sanity/ Healing/ sublimation & More than Music,* where I discussed the psychological effects that music can have on the listener, and how it could move them to a place where they are open to the suggestion of dark maniacal forces. Since I wrote *Reflections of the Son* a new word has entered the hip hop  lexicon: "Demon" is frequently used to describe the dark heartless gangster, serial murderer, or a sexual animal. In *Reflections of the Son* I argued that both White supremacist and urban males were being possessed by an incubus, and they were being brainwashed in their youth before they developed critical thinking skills. And for decades Church leaders have argued about the demonic elements within the hip hop community. It is interesting that Black Males have now taken to calling themselves or each other "Demons." Is this life imitating art or art imitating life?

# MUZIKKK & MURDERTAINMENT

I do not believe that Americans properly understand the power of the art form they call music. We have been led to believe that music is one category of something we call "entertainment," instead of a powerful sonic art form - capable of carrying messages, thoughts, emotions, and ideas through time and space. I do not believe that the English language has a word that accurately defines or describes the power of music, as it relates to its ability affect the human soul and personality. Music is much more than entertainment, it is a teaching tool, a science, a technology for self-improvement, and a weapon. It is something we use to transmit all sort of sensitive information - whether the information is secret, sacred, spiritual, mundane, or complex. It is a teaching tool used  to help babies and adults remember volumes of important cultural knowledge. It is therapeutic, being that we use it to sooth our bodies, minds, and souls. Africans have taught their child using music for thousands of years. And for hundreds of years Black slave used songs to conceal their secret messages.

Music is an art form like no other. Static art forms like sculpture, painting, or performance art (acting or dance), require people to first approach and focus their visual senses on an object, scene, or action before understanding its significance. Music, on the other hand, has the ability to penetrate our consciousness and alter our mood, behavior, or perception - without our willingness to engage it. Static or theatrical art forms require us to look, listen, think, and interpret in order to feel its power. Whereas music does not require anything except that we be in proximity to the sonic waves, and for the audio to register at the correct decibel level.

Music cannot be seen, touched or tasted, yet, it can fully encompass our mental faculties (which controls the physical body) until we are unknowingly swaying to the rhythm or absorbing its message. The power of music is so subtle that even if words don't accompany the melody, cord, or strings a person can be stimulated on the emotional plane. Conversely, harmonic words alone (without instruments) are enough to stir the human soul; this is the most ancient form of music and way to transmit the encyclopedia of cultural information we possess. We see this in the Psalms, and the Qur'an. The Qur'an's melodic sound made it easy for a mostly illiterate population to learn, memorize, and transmit Islamic law.

Furthermore, although the rhythm and message of music seem to be one, they are in reality, distinct and different elements that operate independent of one another. Meaning, a dark maniacal message can be placed over a sweet melodic beat, and vis versa, a dark ominous beat can be accompanied by a beautiful message of optimism and love. Christians have been placing both religious messages to both gangsta Rap and Rock & Roll beats for decades. Whatever the case, all music carries within its message an ideology, or set of ideas; no matter how benign, there is no music that does not try to influence how we think and feel. There is no song made for the sake of simply combining random (meaningless) words with harmony. For example, the national anthems of every country is taught to children in order to fill them with a sense of national identity; anthems are meant to inspire people to be proud of where they come from and who they are.

Billie Holliday did not sing 'Strange fruit' to 'entertain' people, She was routinely threatened by law enforcement not to sing that song. Nina Simone did not sing 'Four women' for the leisure of her audience, but to lament the suffering of Black women. Neo Nazis use music as a tool to  indoctrinate young recruits. There are music artist in third world countries imprisoned and tortured because they are making protest music against their nations leaders and presidents. Music has the potential to shift the national conversation and zeitgeist. Political leaders are finely tuned to "protest music" and artist who rail against the machine and advocate for a counter culture revolution. Artist like:  Bob Dylan, Public Enemy, NWA, Ice T, Ice Cube, Pussy Riot (once imprisoned in Russia),  Kute' Fella (tortured by Nigerian military),  and Bob Marley are some of the notable people who have made a name talking about societies corrupt political leaders. In every country around the world artist are using their music, as a tool of protest, to resist  state oppression and corruption; all of them, in their own way, are trying to make their society a better place through art.

********************

We are living in a period of great diversity within music, particularly hip hop. It has surpassed Rock & Roll as the dominant cultural medium of American (global) pop culture. It is thoroughly embedded into the fabric of European, African, and Latin American mainstream and underground subculture. This is probably one of the most creative eras that Black culture has experienced in the modern time. But whether this diversity ultimately benefits the masses of Black people is yet to be seen. Yes, millionaires are being made everyday, icons rise and fall with each changing season, and Black urban culture is the  global epitome of "cool." But what does this mean to the majority of the people?

Not only is it possible that Black people create and not benefit from  their work, but that Black people create and  can be harmed by their own artistry. The vast majority of Black artist who proceeded this generation did not have the social infrastructure (power), organization  nor wealth to maintain control or ownership of their/our music and image. Not only did they lose control of its creation, representation, impact, and monetization, but were - in many ways -destroyed by the fast lifestyle and habits associated with the music industry.

177

Drug addiction, depression, alcoholism, poverty, or early death often went hand in hand with being a Blues, Jazz, Rock & Roll, Soul, or R & B artist. After pouring their heart, soul, and pain into their music, Black musicians simply did not reap the benefits of their efforts, and Black artist - as a whole - suffered. Most forced to sell their genius for pennies to a predatory industry. But this is part of a long sad saga that continues to plague Black people in a world dominated by powerful white institutions and organized wealth.

In the last five hundred years Black ingenuity in the form of creativity, labor, and skills has always gone to benefit other people, and the modern era is no exception. Culture can be mined like oil, gold or iron ore, and sold on the market; as such, it can be stolen, hoarded, or sold for cheap. Until we understand the value of our collective genius, we will never develop the social infrastructure we need to control the production, distribution, and monetization of our various art forms.

Black people have not reaped the tangible benefits of the various art forms we have created and popularized, beginning with the Blues, Jazz, Rock & Roll, Rap, break dancing, and graffiti. We create beautiful music and then were unable to collectively monetize although these are now global art forms. We are no longer the sole gatekeepers of hip hop culture; which means we are in dangerous territory. The power that the music wields is not solely in our control. If we were intelligent people we would move immediately to consolidate our hold on our cultural markets, art, and image before it is captured, controlled and monopolized by others. We must realize that hip hop culture is more than "entertainment", it is an actual experience and lifestyle. It is a philosophical posture and ideology.

**************

Since the mid-1990s hip hop music and culture has gone mainstream in three separate directions: there is a powerful strain of gangster and gang banging' rap - whose theme is conflict with 'some niggaz,' (opps) and the cops. This nihilistic strain of music focuses on tales of:

178

robbery,
murder,
drug dealing,
drug use,
money, sex,
insanity,
nothingness,
prison,
struggle,
relationships,
loneliness,
family.
There is another strain where the message is dominated by:
money,
materialism,
fashion,
cars,
club life,
blinged-out jewelry,
personal greatness,
relationships,
sex,

Finally, there is a weaker watered down pop hip hop with no substantive message other than to have fun, and to live for the moment. Many rap artist trying to carve out their place in the culture focus on one of these niche markets. However, much of mainstream hip hop is a synthesis of all of these styles and genres. These genres have no substantive political commentary, analysis of society, or critiques of race and power. They are totally devoid of conscious elevating elements. So it is safe to assume that 90% of the dominant cultural expressions of rap lacks any positive, life affirming qualities. Meanwhile, it saturates the Black (and white) psyche with images and messages focused exclusively on ultra materialism, consumerism, death, and sex. Through the medium of rap young Black males are indoctrinated to believe that criminal activity is their exclusive birthright, and  all other Black males, who are not part of their gang, are their enemy and are not to be trusted

Very few rappers with conscious messages have been able to gain real traction and mainstream success. With a  few exceptions, conscious music with scathing political or social commentary and critique is  relegated to the underground. Politically militant music once readily available and abundant is now scarce. It is not for a shortage of material, there are plenty of conscious rappers creating high quality art, but Black males do not want to hear it - and will admit as much.

Conscious rappers  often succeed because they have a small cult following, a  white fan  base, or their message gains momentum outside of the U.S.  Most of the music getting mainstream attention has a  logical coherent core message - even if it is superficial and scatter-brained; some of it is utter nonsense outside of what can be called liberty of art. In fairness, there is good music being made, even if it has the nutritional value of candy. Most mainstream rappers are hoping to maintain street credibility while gaining a more diverse (whiter) demographic fan base, in order to achieve rock star status.

The males  I speak with are open about their aversion  to conscious rap music, they do not want political themes to interfere with their 'drug dealer dreams.' When they speak of 'warfare' they  are not talking about against the 'system'  for righteous  ends, but war against opps, or for turf and their existence as the boss of a criminal network. There are some artist who succeed in inserting conscious themes into their music, nevertheless, their political references are often fleeting and overshadowed by the messages of sociopathic gangsterism, nouveau riche materialism, and  vivid descriptions of sexual activity. When asked: what he "thought  about Black Lives Matter?" one  rapper remarked:

*I am a young Black rich motherfucker...I  don't know what you mean...don't come  at  me  with  that  dumb  ass  shit...My life matter....Especially  to  my  bitches...[interviewer:  do  you  feel connected...?] I don't feel connected to a damn thing that ain't got*

*nothing to do with me. If you do then you crazy as shit." [pulling out his gang flag]... "this matters". 20*

Dismissing a grassroots movement, which advocates for racial equality against police violence, as irrelevant to him. There was much ink spilt over this statement. He was condemned by other artist who were surprised at his words. Shocked that he would say something so crass and shallow at a time, when Black people are getting shot with impunity and feel besieged by their enemies. He basically said: I don't care about Black people. I care about myself and my gang. The same artist used the violent death of Emmett Till in one of his rap songs as a sexual metaphor, and received public backlash for it.

In any case, if there is a rapper who is a absolute nihilist it is him. And people thought that he believed in something righteous, when he has been telling us what he thinks for two decades. As talented as he is, the entire success of his career has been based on rapping about drug use, gangs, and money. He was instrumental in commercializing gang culture and influencing an entire generation of youth to be gangbanging rappers. The same rapper told another reporter on primetime television that he was "a gangster." Oddly enough since the age 13 his life has been lived in the public eye, as a celebrity, which makes it impossible for him to have ever been a real gangbanger or gangster. All he could have ever done was wear some gang colors, learn some slang, and become affiliated with real thugs. There's no-way possible for him to have ever been an actual violent criminal.

'Gangbanging' refers to actually living the life of a hunter and killer of other males accompanied by criminal activity. Gangbanging is a violent lifestyle - period. Whatever else celebrities portray the lifestyle to be is fiction. Rappers have turned gangbanging into posing, posturing, and talking shit because you are initiated into a gang. What is more telling about the aforementioned rapper is that he actually moonlights as a sports commentator on a major network and demonstrates his objective intellectual prowess. I found it strange that in some interviews he fully embraces his thug persona, yet in others he is able to present himself as an articulate and well-studied young man.

I noticed a trend towards cultural nihilism when another rapper (celebrity 'gangbanger') conveyed similar sentiments. The other rapper was asked (on 60 Minutes in front of millions of TV. viewers) if he would snitch: "*if a serial-killer was living next door to him*"? He replied, "*No. I would move away.*" 21  The elevation of these type of personalities as icons has led to the debasement of our culture. They are not alone as artists or as  Black males. There are legions who have been influenced to view the world through a distorted lens. They are a warning to those who fail to acknowledge the shattering of Black America's unified self-perception.

Despite class and cultural differences  present in the community, the murder and abuse of  men,  women, or children  by law enforcement or civilian has always unified Black people, no matter their class. The fact that a major pop artist (in a hostile racial climate) can feel bold enough to dismiss Black lives, as irrelevant, says a lot. For decades artist and sports figures were criticized for remaining silent if they failed to use their voice, platform, and money to support  civil rights; here we have rappers openly saying: *the rest of you mean nothing to me*,  and yet still embraced as icons.


## THE PIED PIPERS OF VANITY AND DEATH


Definition of Pied  Pipers:

1.   One who entices others with delusive promises.

2.   An appealing but irresponsible leader.

Rappers are the new high-priest/tess of the death-sex-materialism cults, that are modern gangs. The Uber drug-kingpins and violent killers are cultural idols; and verses, hymns,  odes, and songs of praise are written to and about them. This gives new meaning to the Rick Ross track: *"idols become rivals."* Anyone who believes that music is only entertainment has never  thought of the subject seriously. The word "entertainment" is not powerful enough to capture the psychic relationship that exist between an artist and their fans. The artist becomes the living embodiment of an ideal (saint, gangster, killer, mogul, prophet, or god/dess). Artist both channel and become physical representations of a concept; these are powerful personas that are revered, adored, and obeyed.

If they say 'wear this brand,' they are followed; if they say 'this person is the enemy,' they are believed; if they say 'this drink is good for you,' it will be consumed; if they say sex should be performed like this, it will be emulated; if they say you are nothing without this kind of car,  their followers feel insecurity until they have it.  If they say 'go here this is where the fun is,' people will flock to that destination. There is no direction that an artist cannot take their fans or followers, who are quasi-disciples. Like any perverted religion, they create the sickness and then claim to be the cure. I believe some of this music is responsible for neurosis, particularly among males. Between the music and social media our children (male and female) are developing dangerous insecurities.

Female artist like Sade, Jill Scott, and Eryka Badu transcend the ordinary to their fans. They are not women, they are ideals. They are the ultimate woman, or more precisely, the ultimate feminine spirit. Those who listen to them want a priestess to use her voice to connect them to a deeper truth. Sade has cultivated a spiritual mystique like no other female artist. I don't know of any artist whose name and music is mentioned with such reverence - among men and women. Tupac Shakur recounted in one of his books how national gang leaders wanted him to be the leader of their movement, and wanted to hand him authority over tens of thousands of foot soldiers. Until this episode Shakur had no idea he possessed this type of power  over his disciples. To his disciples Tupac embodied the ultimate gangster spirit.

Idolatry is difficult to up root in any population, people will defend their favorite artist like pagans defend their wooden and stone statues. If you tell a young person that the music is negatively effecting them they immediately become defensive and place a psychological barrier up. It is not to say that there would be no evil without music. People would still do really dumb shit and wicked things without the influence of music, but the music cannot be seen as a neutral force or energy in cultivating dark gangster and gangstress personas. There is a real connection between drill artist (around the world) and violence; it is not a coincidence that rappers who talk about killing enemies are killing enemies and are being killed themselves.

Music transmits ideas, emotions, and philosophies whether they be good, bad, or ugly. The dangerousness  of music comes from its inability to be controlled. The best (most positive) or  worst (morally depraved) messages can be merged with the most seductive beat or image, and carried into the soul of a person without resistance. Furthermore, a person can extract from the artist what they want, as is done with Tupac. Those who want to hear the righteous message have much to take from, and those who want to hear the gangster /nihilist have all the content they need.

Black people are the only group fed the lie that music has no value outside its entertainment value. Or is this a convenient conversation ender when the subject of rap music's negative message and image  comes up? Those who believe music can soothe the mind, and heal the soul, must admit that anything with the power to heal also has the power to hurt. *"Plato [believed] that nothing could more strongly influence man's innermost feeling than melody and rhythm."22* According to *Confucius: to educate somebody, you should start with poems, emphasize ceremonies, and finish with music.* Ancient armies used music to induce a collective warrior ethos into its soldiers. Music is used to drill men and women in preparation for military combat. According to Greek sources:

*Both Isis and Osiris were patrons of music and poetry. Plato, in describing the antiquity of these arts among the Egyptians, declared that songs and poetry had existed in Egypt for at least ten thousand years, and that these were of such an exalted and inspiring nature that only gods or godlike men could have composed them. 23*

Music is a very potent theme in many fairytales and myths dealing with deception and seduction. The medieval story of the 'pied piper' is a perfect analogy. It focuses on a man who had been cheated by town leaders and returned to lead the town's children away from their village - presumably to death. He is often depicted as using a flute or fiddle to lure the children away. The children lured by the sweet melody go willingly to their death while dancing to a tune. This demonstrates that ancient thinkers understood that music could be used to entice young minds, who couldn't discern the intentions of those they were following. Another myth where music is the instrument of death is in the Greek myth of the sirens, whose music and sweet voice called sailors to their death. Men were supposed to cover their ears when in proximity of these beautiful maidens who sat on rocky shores. Music is considered such a harmful force in Islam that the prophet Muhammad said all but a few instruments were haram (forbidden) for Muslims to listen to.

It is well known that rappers Foxy Brown and Little Kim transformed the self-perception of an entire generation of young women. When I first heard these artist I knew that the style and mentality of inner city females was forever changed. At the height of their popularity every girl in the street was emulating these rappers; from their dress to their attitude. To witness the proliferation of colorful wigs among young girls was enough to see that Kim's effect on them was immediate. Foxy Brown and Little Kim told young females they could be gangsters too, and that their bodies were both weapons that could be used to lure men into a trap and instrument for their personal pleasure. Neither of these artist EVER spoke about motherhood and the value of the womb as man's first temple, or giving birth to prophets or leaders. Neither spoke about raising families or spirituality. None of them had any political commentary in their music. They told girls that all that mattered was designer clothes, hand bags, rich men, jewelry, and nice cars. They laid out the blueprint for future female artist; who realized that mediocre female artist could get attention if they followed this gangtress / slut road map.

The irony is this, the words of Kim were not even her own. They were words and ideas of males being put into her mouth. Kim was not articulating her own thoughts, she was rapping something written for her, or writing raps other people wanted to hear. Manipulative and predatory males created Kim's Trap queen character for their own financial gain; this is the same persona that little girls emulated. This was never an authentic feminine voice. The men writing for Little Kim and Foxy were using them like a ventriloquist uses a dummy. Speaking to an audience of our girls using female artist as puppets. Kim was Biggie's puppet, Biggie was Puff Daddy's puppet, Puff Daddy was the puppet of the faceless (white) executives who cut his checks.

I am not saying that white executive were responsible for the premeditated moral decay of our youth, I am saying that these white executive don't personally care what our children are ingesting or what it is doing to them, as long as the executives make money. Whereas the Black executives are more culpable because they really understand the culture, and know they are pushing a morally corrupting message. There are now hundreds of male and female executives following Puffy's blueprint. And Kim and Foxy have been replaced by a new generation of raunchy artist, who cannot get any attention unless they over-sexualize themselves, and promote hedonism.

Through music (lyrics, rhymes, and video) and urban culture the adolescent female consciousness is penetrated by a malevolent male spirit. Which grafts itself to her subconscious and assumes command over her logic and world view. Her movements, gaze, speech and gestures take on masculine affectations or expectations. She will either become a caricature of a male or female.

In other words, she will assume a masculine persona, or become the embodiment of a sexually aggressive male's desire - whatever that looks like to her. In either case she is a cartoon. Notice that girls are acutely interested in what boys think or discuss among themselves. However, males don't generally care what girls are doing or thinking. Girls want to know so they can adjust and calibrate their behavior to be accepted as an equal or ideal fantasy.

Women, on the other hand, seek a deeper communion with themselves and their own power. They command respect from men because of who they are, not because of who men want them to be. They don't need the male gaze because their own is complete. What little girls hear when they listen to most female rappers is actually the personality of an incubus or male demon, masquerading behind a female voice.

Males started talking about king-pin drug dealing and then females started rapped about it; male rappers started rapping about murder, then female artist followed; males rapped about gangs and drilling and then female artist followed suit; male artist talk about sexual conquest and female artist joined in. Little girls learn this from their environment, or by tapping into the music and culture. I can't count how many females rappers are now rapping about violence; female artist are now talking about "*spinning the block to catch an opp*", and throwing up gang signs.

These are NOT authentic feminine personas, they are corporately manufactured characters. Just look at the contorted faces, attitude, and posture of today's female rappers, they are the attributes of a mentally unstable male, or male possessed by a demon. Nicky Minaj's alter ego Roman was a clear manifestation of this schizoid personality. The only thing about female rappers that indicate feminine traits are their tight clothes, naked bodies, and grossly exaggerated proportions. If you were to put clothes on female rappers and allow them to rap the same lyrics, all traces of femininity would vanish - as is the case of Young MA who does not dress provocatively. These personas are so masculine that whenever it is announced that one of these artist is pregnant it seems strange. 'How can a dude have a baby?' is what the subconscious asks. Foxy Brown, Little Kim, and Nicky Minaj do not conjure thoughts of motherhood to males; they are marketed as objects for sexual gratification, their pregnancy seems ridiculous.

Not only has the perception of females changed for adolescent girls, but also for adolescent boys. Adolescent boys now come of age and see ALL women as succubus, waiting to ensnare him with their voice, body, clothes, and sex. Males are now trained to see all women as devils in a blue Louis Vuitton dress and Gucci bag. And where did he learn this? Well, from those artist who speak for women, of course. Men don't want to marry Medusa – he wants to escape her glare, subdue her, or kill her.

These artist know their personas are manufactured; while others, so brainwashed by materialism, push this lifestyle unconsciously. They don't actually have to be manipulated as adults, because they have been indoctrinated as children to accept that their status is linked to what they have. Rapper Rubi Rose is a perfect example of a manufactured persona, a beautiful young woman whose parents are doctors and lawyers, she dropped out of law school to pursue a music career. Among the themes of her music are unfiltered sexual references, references to gang culture, and wanting a thug nigga for a man. Her music comes off like she was raised in a ghetto by a 'Trap Queen.' Contrary to her ratchet nymphomaniac persona, in interviews, she speaks about wanting a good man who is faithful and how she abhors unfaithful men and only believes in monogamy. The image she presents in her music, as authentic, is a complete façade. The number male artist guilty of the same thing cannot be quantified.

Music transmits ideas, emotions, and philosophies whether they are good, bad, or ugly. The dangerousness of music comes from its inability to be controlled. The best (most positive) or worst (morally depraved) message can be merged with the most seductive beat or image, and carried into the soul of a person without resistance.

Like putting poison in chocolate. Furthermore, a person can extract from the artist what they want, as is done with Tupac.

During a conversation with another male we both realized that we liked the rock band Soundgarden. When their song entitled: '*Blackhole Sun*' came up, the male (who was white) said something to the effect: "*Man, that song makes you...,*" he was struggling to articulate his feelings. At this point I continued the thought for him: "*it makes you want to kill somebody,*" and he said "Yeah!"

How is it that two people from different backgrounds can be moved to the same psychological and emotional plane by the same song? What is even more strange is that I really don't know the words to the song. The strings, rhythm, melody, and voice of the singer are haunting enough to induce sadness and rage. The lead singer of the band killed himself in 2017. But it has been  said that 'all the best rock & roll artist die young.' It is common knowledge that it is a world beset by genius, drugs, depression,  alcoholism, and hedonism. Hip Hop is similarly plagued by these issues - in addition to - prison, murders, and shootings.

I listen to many forms of music (Hardcore gangsta Rap included), but I am fully aware of what the various genres do for me. I know where I want to go on the emotional spectrum and I use music to reach a particular mental state, whether it is relaxation or rage. I approach music with respect of its power and I know what I want from it before I turn it on. That said, I  believe that most of the mainstream Hip Hop being created is not appropriate for children. A child of 6, 8, 10, 12, or 14  (boy or girl) and a 30 year old gangster or stripper should not be listening to the same music. Themes of graphic violence, murder, sex, and deception should not be introduced to the adolescent imagination before they have reached a certain level of maturity, self-control, and discernment. Anyone letting their child listen to today's music is guilty of neglect and corrupting the morals of a child.

While a generation of young males was listening to Scarface's dark tales  for criminal inspiration (It was the "drill" music of the 1990s) Scarface was denying (In the Diary/ 1994) that rap had a negative effect on people. However, J. Prince (King-pin turned Rap executive)  founder of Rap-A-Lot records, who introduced Scarface and the Ghetto Boyz to the world, admitted in his autobiography, that he did not allow his own young children to listen to rap.

In any case, all of the rappers hiding behind the "entertainer" label are liars. They know the power they have and use it went they want. The designation of 'entertainer' is used to avoid social responsibility and liability for the lives they destroy and people they lead astray: *I did not tell you to sell drugs, I am only an entertainer; I didn't tell you to kill, I'm only an entertainer; I didn't tell you to join a gang, I'm only an entertainer; I didn't tell you to prostitute your self for a handbag,  I'm only an entertainer.*

Rapper Malice (one of two brothers) of the rap group Clipse retired from the industry  in 2012 and became a born again Christian. The Clipse had made their image and money rapping about being drug pushers and violence. In many interviews he explained that he knew that the music they were making was harmful  and that it was negative and dangerous. In response to a question about Tupac Shakur rapping about death in his music shortly before dying, Malice told Vlad TV: *"I do believe we can speak death upon ourselves......How many times people went to jail listening  to the things that I was saying? How many times somebody's head was blown out and the theme music was still playing."*

The union between Hip Hop, gangsterism, and American pop culture is consummated; this unification has been taking place for decades. Together they have given birth to a deformed culture where music, art, creativity, consumerism, and criminality (and everything that comes with it) are intertwined. Social media has accelerated communication and exchanged  of ideas and creativity between humanity, in a way that cannot be measured.  Social media has evolved while Hip Hop has been ascendant as a cultural force, so it has become one of  the mediums   through which Hip Hop  culture is expressed.

Hip Hop as a culture is made up of three parts:  sound (rap), style, and image (look).  It is a culture that is expressed through action - people must be moving, gesturing, or posing. Therefore the visual depiction of Hip Hop is reflected on the body through hair, clothing, jewelry, attitude, posture, and dance.  Where there is the sound, there is the image of the culture. When you see someone who listens to rap you know they listen to rap. Not only do they have a style of dress, but their sound and movement is urban. Take away the jewelry, clothes, and sound, and their posture would give them away. Take away their posture, and their clothes or sound would give them away.

Hip Hop culture is a philosophically diverse; there is no particular belief system that can define people who listen to Rap. People who listen to the music can fit anywhere on the political or ideological spectrum.  That said, Rap has origins among the urban poor and politically disenfranchised minorities, therefore it is both the sound of a counter culture and an angry subculture. Because artists often come from impoverished conditions, criminality is a potent force within the culture. It is particularly intertwined with music artist and lower level executives. Rap/ Hip Hop culture is a very alluring, visible, and imposing culture. Where there is the image (look) there is the culture (the behavior); where there is the culture there is materialism; where there is materialism there is greed; where there is greed there is crime; where there is crime there is gangsterism; and where there is gangsterism there is murder. In this case murdertainment.

# MASSTER MEDIA

The mainstream media has never been a friend to Black people, it is the first and oldest medium used to denigrate our name, character, and image. If we had supporters they have always been those on the (radical) periphery of American politics and media. By media I mean: any individual or group who conveys information (facts, figures, opinion, philosophy, ideology, entertainment) by way of  digital, theatrical, print, audio, or video medium - for profit or social agenda. The masster media is a machine used to inform,  transform,  mold, and shape public opinion - that is its primary function.

Mastering the art of transmitting grand illusions is the masster media's specialty. Presenting images and information of the human condition that are intentionally out of focus is the goal. Reality (or truth) that is too ugly is absent, messages that are too complicated are never conveyed. The entire media infrastructure (global, national, or local) is a polished and stylized manipulation of reality - designed to subtly penetrate our senses, with maximum effect. 'Black media' is no exception.

Through the media (News networks, print media, entertainment, cinema, internet) the  male receives his brainwashing. He is an absolute slave to the images that are projected at him. The majority of his innermost desires stem from the impressions made upon him from the sounds and images created at the behest of corporations, or independent manipulators who, themselves, are influenced by corporate massters. For decades network television and music videos provided the Black male and female with their daily dose of fantasy. Now, they are besieged from every direction, of social media, by illusions of gangsta glamour and "lifestyles of the rich and shameless."

It may be that male biology, fatherless homes, poverty, and weak intellect make the urban male more susceptible to manipulation by corporate propaganda than any other group. The depiction of hip hop culture created by those in the industry is tailored to appeal to the psychological proclivities of the urban male. He and his  money and jewelry are the stars of the show, and females, cars and haters are supporting cast members. His day dreams of infinite wealth, with little or no effort, appeals to the rolling stone nature of  urban mentality. He actually sees 'reality television' or reality internet as reality itself. He wants to be acknowledged and respected, but respect to him means being feared; being a gangster and killer is his idea of being a man. He wants the shiny things he sees, he wants the women, he wants to be a playboy. He just does not want to work hard or sacrifice for them. If it is not presented to him bathed in glitter, glam, or gore it is obsolete. He equates being versed in pop-culture trivia and consumer advertisement info with substantive knowledge. Who is sleeping with who, in the entertainment industry, and the price of the new Lamborghini or Rolex is treated as equivalent, or more important, than knowledge of science, business, law, mathematics, and history.

The Black female is no different, she too engages in escapism, but her day dreams are more modest. She does not want to be a superstar, known killer or feared by her peers. She only wants to be an upper middleclass white woman. Black women want to be socialites who own their own homes, drive luxury cars, possess designer bags and shoes, and take trips to foreign destinations. She wants to look important and be seen. She also wants to be present at all the big events, accompanied by her entourage of  inferior friends. But above all she desires to have a faithful husband who can complement her material and intellectual status, and satisfy her sexually. She wants to be wanted and loved.

The Black women does not want anyone to perceive her as struggling, and goes out her way to create the façade that she has much more than she actually does. Black women will go broke trying to portray themselves as rich. Many are not above employing criminal means to maintain this illusion. On average the Black woman is more educated, mature, and sophisticated than the average Black male.  If not hampered by child rearing (single-handedly) they would surpass the average Black male through work ethic, hustle, and grit alone.

The rise of social media has made access to and production of 'entertainment' instantly available to a younger audience. The playing field has been leveled, now even ordinary people (young and old) are creating their own content. Social media is the place where young men and women jostle for recognition, respect, and attention. They go to social media to be seen, heard, and connect. The ordinary person is empowered, they do not have to look up at celebrities to see a star they can look in the mirror. They don't have wait to see themselves depicted by "professionals", they now participate in the making and distribution of their own content and image. They do not wait to be entertained, they actively take part in the generation and presentation of their culture to the world.

The growth of this technology and people power has resulted in the production of some very impressive media, art, and new cultural expression. From the comfort of home they are writers, actors, commentators, interviewers, opinion makes, producers, analyst, directors, editors, and publishers of their own entertainment. People's dogs, gardens, children, parents, cars, crazy neighbors, friends, spouses, relationships, skin, hair, new clothes, music, and vacations are the subjects of endless posts, tweets, podcasts, and videos. Inexpensive technology that are both intuitive and accessible to all has made the world flat and easy to traverse. Black Twitter is a Black intellectual's dream come true, Black people's innermost thoughts can be observed and documented in real time. The popular terms are "influencers" or culture leaders. The level of human interaction and cultural synthesis is truly impressive and revolutionary.

Professional artist and media personalities have leveraged themselves within this revolutionary media landscape. Rappers, singers, gangster, dancers, DJs, producers, and radio personalities have their own channels, Podcasts, consumer products, clothing lines, sneaker brands, wines, spirits, beverages, headphones, speakers, video games, and social justice causes. They are now consulted by luxury clothing-brand designers, National sports leagues and marketing teams for all sorts of products. Young Black artist also play a more active role behind the scenes as directors, writers, and producers.

The down side of this new found power is that even the most desperate and depraved content is present at the surface of the culture. As it pertains to Hip Hop culture, much of what is created is benign, mostly insider gossip mongering, or salacious behind-the-scenes exposé interviews; no damage is done except that the consumer's time is squandered. Some of what is being produced is truly positive, in the form of analysis and critiques of the culture, and true representations of Hip Hop's historic artistry, diversity, and complexity. However, much of it represents a race to the bottom. For decades the Black male was unfairly presented to the world as a buffoon or volatile; an unhinged menace to American society. Now with the new technology of social media Black males present themselves to the world as a volatile buffoon; by his own words and actions he appears to support the idea that he is an unhinged menace to American society.

In fact, much of the burgeoning technology with limitless applications is being used by many for base motivations (gossip, lying, slander, to sow beef, and posing), to entertain, and self-delusion (escapism). Many of the rivalries, assaults, fights, and murders of high school students or between girls, gangs, or crews can be traced back, in real time, to their origins on social media. Through facebook & Instagram the public and law enforcement can now see the actual beginning of the antagonism that led to a murder or assault. The Black male no longer has to watch music videos and daydream about being rich, a criminal, or playboy; he can create his own videos where he is the director and star. Those who aspire to a life of crime can learn from the safety of home; where they can absorb - through all the senses - the latest slang, lingo, facts, fads, brands, poses, and swags. Even if he is not associated with a gang he can, nevertheless, perfect the appearance of being affiliated. Through rap lyrics and imagery the young person can emerge from their cocoon in the suburbs and assume the persona of a thug. Draped in the right hairstyle, form fitting clothes, and tattoos a person who knows nothing about the underworld can appear to be fully immersed.

Those with real affiliations can demonstrate their money and infamy to their regional fan base, until  they are indicted, and their digital footprint is used as evidence against them. For many criminals, posting on and monitoring social media is an irresistible part of their daily activity. No matter how indictable his behavior is he must broadcast, via video, audio, or text, his life in real time. Because underneath that tough guy/girl persona is a person who just wants to be famous - for anything! So desperate and thirsty are some for fame that live streaming murders, confessions to murder, or recording themselves next to dead bodies, has become the latest way of remaining relevant.

There is even an entire industry of social media created to document, monitor, critique, and monetize this criminal activity. The social media content of rappers and their criminal associates is now scrutinized by companies and independent personalities post by post, image by image, and frame by frame; there are thousands of Facebooks pages, Twitter pages, Podcasts, blogs, Youtube channels, documentaries, and Instagram pages, dedicated to discussing and dissecting cryptic statements, rap lyric "confessions", fights, assaults, and gangland murders. Now the underworld origins of every gang set, gang leader,  goon, serial killer, assassin, king pin, and hit man is set to its own sound track, dialogue, and commentary.

Slick cutting-edge editing is used to make cinematic films out of the lives of local drug dealers and high school dropouts. Petty criminals, with severe drug addictions, are elevated to notorious national figures who run the most infamous urban jurisdictions in America. Males who cannot afford a private attorney are portrayed as if they are in control of all of the lucrative criminal activity in a particular territory - when they can barely feed themselves, their families, or venture out of their own areas.

Crime is not the only thing being analyzed in the Hip Hop culture - fashion, celebrity gossip, relationships and the music quality is also thoroughly commented on. However, the criminal aspect of the culture is so potent that it generates much of the attention by youth and critics of the culture. "Controversy sells" and this mantra is fully embraced by rap artists and those trying to make a name for themselves within the industry. Those who seek attention, by any means, are labeled: "Clout chasers." They will say and do anything to get the attention they crave. And since negativity generates more buzz, clout chasers do and say anything that brings more infamy. For males bricks of money and violence is their gateway to recognition, whereas sex, skin, and grotesque proportions opens all doors for females.

The state of modern entertainment is such that content must reach new levels of outrageousness just to grab and keep attention. This outrageousness is taken as the universal norm by those youth who are raised on these images. The behavior is also taken by many as authentic - especially by the very young. Because it is seen as authentic, those moving toward maturity and adulthood  feel as if they must conform to what they see portrayed in order to be normal. When young people see other people becoming popular and rich by acting violent, strange, or crazy they believe this is the recipe for success. And follow these patterns of behavior hoping to achieve their own fame. How many generations of young men were mislead thinking that Tupac embodied true masculinity? Now young women have their own idols to worship.

Those without strong family foundations that provide good training and counter narrative are seduced by the allure of decadence. Those without the ability to isolate or block these detrimental images before their young children succumb to the propaganda, run a high risk of their children being brainwashed during the adolescent stage of development. Where the children create self-fulfilling prophecies from the poison they have ingested through their eyes and ears. The media never relents and never stops imposing itself on the mind; and for this reason they enter a self-perpetuating loop where reality is lost behind a thick smoke of illusion; in this world fiction, lies, and the absurd become pathologically important.

There are consequence to all of these paradigms of religion, gang culture, music, and media that cause alienation between the Black male and the Black community. Black males are fanatically embracing ideas and concepts that distort his perception of reality and pit him against the larger community. Black males are operating by belief systems which set him on a path of utter backwardness. He is actually sacrificing himself for everyone and everything except his family and community. His time, energy, and life are wasted chasing the wind, and leaving a trail of bodies in his wake. For profit and power he has abandoned civilization for barbarism.

When racial strife inevitably surges in America, these males have no historical or logical context which to analyze the phenomenon. They have no concept of "us" except as victims or a vague amorphous body of humans that bad stuff happens to. Without a clear philosophical context no people can develop a strategy to confront their opposition. You cannot approach problems or solve them if you do not clearly see them. When Black people are shot, some Muslims see nothing but a 'disbeliever', while the gangbanger only sees 'some niggah over there'; neither sees a 'brother' or 'sista' or 'us.' Let me provide an example, while this section was being revised there was a mass shooting in Buffalo, New York where Black people were the target of a racist killer. I asked myself what criticism of this shooting can a gang banger really offer, when he himself lives a violent existence and Blacks are his primary targets? What can he say to the white supremacist who hates Blacks just as much as he does? This is what I mean by consequences to our philosophical beliefs. How can you solve problems for yourself if your current belief system does not recognize the problems  actually existence?

I have seen it on so many occasions, some big traumatic event happens and the Black male is at a loss for words. He cannot contextualize white supremacist violence when his own celebration of death is equally perverse. How can he condemn a mass shooter when he celebrates this sort of spectacle of violence against his own opps. Young kids getting shot in the streets brings strange looks and blank stares to young Black males. How can he feel sympathy when he shoots at people in residential areas as well? Probe their mind after some event. The Black male has no in-depth critique, he can only say "that's crazy," or "that's fucked up." Yet when somebody that looks like him is shot by the police he sees the injustice clearly.

# SLEEP NO MORE

I began writing this book in 2016, based off my observations of Black males and his psychology. I focused on the prison population because my time in prison had given me a unique opportunity to observe the Black male in his most vulnerable state. His entire belief system was revealed to me over the course of two decades. I was able to watch, follow, and hear from the old and the young, and take stock of their world view. During this period I was also able to document the evolution of my own beliefs.

When I began contemplating the topics in this book my outlook was bleak, the males I observed were in a very strange state of being. Political awareness was at an all-time low and gang infatuation was high. Since I began writing I had to revise sections of the book to update it with current information. As I grew and my perspective expanded so did the book. I have always wanted to present a text that was honest and accurate, as it pertains to the Black male's flawed concept of history and how that relates to his perception of himself. After the death of Travon Martin (2012) I noticed a new conscious awakening among the old and young which gave me hope that the young people were not lost.

Writing LEGACY & INHERITANCE enhanced my understanding of social consciousness. I realize that political awareness is something that ebbs and flows; populations who are dead can be revived, but they can also go back to sleep. Although people may wake up from their sleep and become active, it does not mean they will develop intelligent strategies. Without strong leaders, the political awareness and energy of a population will be wasted pursuing symbolic objectives, that fail to address the true causes of their problems. Just as there is a period of confusion after waking from a real deep sleep, there is also a period of confusion after waking from political slumber. It is during this period of confusion that (good or bad) leaders appear.

I have come to understand that young people lack an in-depth understanding of history in general and Black history in particular. They are not aware of our great Black thinkers or the body of literature about the Black experience. They have little understanding of our recent achievements or legacy. This made me realize that beneficial knowledge can be lost or erased from memory in a very short period of time. Furthermore, the current racial awareness of young people does not have a strong racial pride component to it, like generations of the 70s, 80s, and 90s; rather, their activism seems to rest on a foundation of racial resentment. They are not motivated from a feeling of Black optimism and hope, but despair and despondency.

They do not seek Black power in the way past leaders envisioned, they want recognition of Black suffering. They do not envision a bright future where we build a Black nation within a nation, from the descendants of slaves; or a Diaspora movement where Blacks are tightly linked culturally and economically. The world is dark to young people, everything is bad, and nobody can be trusted; psychologically, they are fighting from a defensive posture. For them Black people's only connection is our common victimization, it is the only concept they have to bind 'us' together. In short, the "we" for young people is "we the victims." Not "we" the sovereign people or "we" the Black citizens who must fix our situation.

Travon Martin's death lit a fire under young people who had been in a propaganda induced sleep. In ten years I have witnessed a growing sense of a collective self-awareness among young people.

They are no longer afraid to bring up race or injustice in their analysis of a situation. Modern social justice activists are becoming more vocal and visible; the size of the crowds that get out in the streets is proof that young people want to be organized and led. The people realize the issues we face cannot be conquered alone. Much of this new sense of political awareness is encouraged by young  men and women of many backgrounds and races. The activism of young people on the left is encouraging, their energy is contagious, although some of their strategies and goals may be misguided.

There is also a powerful strain of Black nationalism among the young. Although young people have what are clearly Black nationalist beliefs they don't call themselves black nationalist. If you listen you will hear them talk of only supporting Black businesses, buying land, not dating outside the race, and building Black communities, and hostility towards outsiders. But they will not cite Booker T. Washington, Marcus Garvey, Elijah Muhammad, or the hundreds of Black people who laid the foundation for Black nationalism on American soil. Many of whom go unstudied or acknowledged. Young people speak about subjects as if they thought of them all by themselves, or as if they are new revelations. This generation are under the impression that nobody understands their world, and that they are unique and special. When nothing can be further from the truth. The blueprints left by our leaders were not flawed, rather, it was the men left to execute the building of the proper institutions that failed. Black leaders of the 19th & 20th century lived in a modern world; the strategies and ideas they developed for our survival are still sound. They did not let us down we let them down.

While young people have great talking points, they proceed without a blueprint because they will not reference our scholars and leaders and follow the road maps left behind. They are not as well read because all of their learning is based on sound bites and cursory reading; which has replaced research and methodical examination. Before the prevalence of personal computers and smart phones every generation in pursuit of knowledge had to get their information from books; they had no choice but to read all relevant text on a given subject in order to become proficient in the field. By this very fact they were engaged in the analysis and examination of hundreds of authors and thinkers. This means past leaders and laymen were brilliant men and women, familiar with all relevant sides of a debate when they engaged in discussion. They were not debating a fragment of a quote they heard that day on a post, made by a hair-dresser.

Young people are used to digital information, which makes them short in attention span and not well versed in the classics. They learn from Posts, Tweets, and internet browsing, not deep reading and reflection. Young people can sit behind a screen and be a keyboard activist whereas past generations had to get dirty, hurt, arrested, and killed for their beliefs. Who are the modern equivalents to Elijah Muhammad, Malcolm X, Stokely Carmichael, Assata Shakur, Elaine Brown, Huey Newton, Fannie Lou Hammer, Martin Luther King, Louis Farrakhan, H. Rap Brown, and the hundreds of unknown men and women who sacrificed their wealth, and lives for a better tomorrow?

The three decades of the 50s, 60s, and 70s saw the greatest concentration of Black genius and revolutionary activism in American history. It was a golden age of Black thought. Where are the successors to these people? Where has the spirit of these people gone? The fact that there seems to be no need for them is proof that they left a better world then they found. Yes, we have an abundance of millionaires, professionals, writers, intellectuals, celebrities, professional talkers but these people do not hold a torch to our greatest generations of revolutionaries. We have too many law professors to count, but have no leaders to guide us and direct our boundless energy.

I can see it and hear it in everyday discourse, young people want a new world. They don't want to hate, or discriminate, they want to thrive. They have all the information at their fingertips but they have no one to guide them. Nobody is going to tell them we have to wait for things to get better when they can see the tools and resources for a better tomorrow all around them. They are right to feel impatient about progress when they can see all the ingredients for revolution in front of them; the circulation of massive global wealth, international telecommunication infrastructure, high-speed global travel, technology capable of extraordinary engineering feats, abundance of food, available land, innovative textile fabrication, and revolutions in energy production. Nations of the world have the capacity to feed cloth, house, and raise millions out of poverty and ignorance, if only the right people are put in the right positions. Even third world citizens are walking around with private super computers in their pockets. A young woman today in the Congo has the same internet access and information as a fortune 500 CEO. They can both find the answer to any question in a matter of seconds.

It is impossible to overlook the dominant role of women in keeping our people conscious and in taking the fight to the empire. Behind much of this activism, protest, and the grassroots organizing are old and young women fed up with the state of affairs. They are spearheading much of the political agitation and intellectual ground work. They are overrepresented in mass protest and underappreciated for their effort. When Black males are getting shot it is women on the frontline demanding that 'Black Lives Matter.' They are carrying the people when they can, and dragging us when they must. They have no equal in terms of resilience and resistance. Black women are keeping Black consciousness alive. In many cases they are much more stable than their male counterparts. The collective Black female working and professional classes  have inherited the work load, but not the infrastructure of our past leaders.

They are overburdened taking care of the broken down Black family, which has been left shattered by Black male criminality, addiction, and irresponsibility. I believe Black women are always ready to take part in a social revolution; they are energetic, educated, and restless. We (males) are not being hampered by them, they are being held back by our inability to mature into stable responsible men. Male inability or unwillingness to meet them halfway or even stand on our own is the primary cause of family instability or dysfunction. The urban Black male is a needy figure, who seems to exist in a perpetual state of dependence. So much so that society has institutionalized its low expectations of his abilities and actual potential. Every social structure is operating off the notion that the Black male is below average in intelligence and common sense.

************

Christians are also highly visible in organizing, Black preachers are masters at inciting rebellion in the hearts of the masses. They are comfortable using race as an organizing factor as they have since the plantation. The influence of Black church on the community or family life may fluctuate but it will not disappear anytime soon - nor should it; it is an institution in need of spiritual, organizational, and political reform. When church leaders model their behavior after prophets instead of politicians they will achieve the first step towards organizing Black communities. Everything that needs to be done to build a community from scratch is found in scripture. Everything needed to build an aggressive social uplift movement and parallel economic strategy is rooted in scripture. It is simply a matter of reading scripture like we are masters of earth instead of slaves of men.

We must recognize first and foremost that the Black church is not a monolithic institution, we must stop thinking of the church as one big thing. There are literally tens of thousands of leaders and millions of members with their own territory and agenda. There are men a women of the cloth that are fighting the good fight. They are using their resources to preach, teach, organize, and heal; they are doing gods works as instructed by the prophets. Who do we think is consoling the thousands of grieving mothers whose children are being gunned down or overdosing in these streets? Who is performing funeral rites of drug dealers, gang members, drug addicts and the elderly for cheap when their loser friends or family can't pay for caskets or burial plots?

205

The Black church is the community that mothers turn to when their families have been decimated from drugs, death, and prison. When our mothers are old and their beauty has faded, and their families are scattered, and their neighbors are corrupt, and their children neglect them, and they are alone, they turn to the church and to other mothers who know what they are going through. The Black church gets a bad name because very often high profile leaders are caught in sexual or money scheme scandals. When in truth these people don't represent the majority of church leaders, who have good intentions, however, are poor and operate in very distressed areas on very tight budgets. Their loaves of bread are few but sliced very thin in order to feed the legions of invisible destitute and needy.

The sleep is also over for young Muslims; they are not the blind followers their elders were, and are suspicious of the old order. They will not allow themselves to be divided from everyone else. When Muslims are targeted by the government they cannot fail to see the outpouring of support they receive from non-Muslims. They have also seen the kind of world that emerges when fanatics use Islam to commit unspeakable crimes. No matter how foreign leaders posture themselves ideologically Islam in America will never resemble Saudi Arabia. American institutions are too liberal and the people are too free and too armed. There is no way to institutionalize fundamentalism in a population like ours. Being as such young Muslims understand that their problems cannot be separated from the rest of humanity. They will either struggle with the rest of us or be classified as unwitting dupes of foreign agents.

I have heard enough from this generation to see they are critical of the corrupting music; they are exhausted from the gang violence; they are tired of the peer pressure of social media. Through social media they mock rappers, gangs, and the worst aspects of our culture. Today's young men and women are smart; their eyes are open and they want answers that will satisfy them in this life. They are not going to sit on the sidelines imagining their struggles are separate from the rest of their brothers and sisters. They are tired of the lame excuses of today's Black intellectuals of why we are in dire circumstances. Black America's problems don't stem from wealth gaps with whites, lack of educational opportunities, or segregated schools; they are the result of a longstanding and debilitating leadership crisis.

With the right leaders in charge and guided by the right philosophy and principles even a modest size group of (10,000) men and women can cover the economic and intellectual ground of a million. The entire federal government of the United States (population 360,000,000) is run by only 2.1 million federal employees; the DOD the executive branch department in charge of the U.S. military is staffed by 750,000 civilians; the U.S. military has only 1.3 million active service members, 810, 000 national guard reserve, 3,000 non-defense personnel, and 600, 000 private sector employees; the Pentagon which is the country's military command center and brain is staffed by 23, 000 civilian and military personnel; furthermore the U.S. military industrial complex is a global organism not a domestic institution. All in all very few people are responsible for the most sophisticated and powerful military structure to have ever existed. These few million people and the weapons they control and logistics capabilities they have can make the entire earth of 7, 000, 000, 000 shake. Even America's system of higher education is impressive by its numbers. There are roughly 5,300 colleges and universities in America and around 135, 000 college professors- which are about evenly split between men and women; who oversee the pedagogical responsibility of tens of millions of global students.

It is self-evident that endowed with the gift of insight, rationality, science, and superior organization a small group can do the work of a group twenty times their size. We can see this on the family level where one or two family members are the backbone of a family of two dozen. I believe that a hundred thousand (fearless & competent) men and women working in a unified and concerted effort can change the direction of 45 million Blacks in America. We are missing thousands of virtuous leaders and people of inspiration needed to focus and organize millions of restless souls. We have to the raw material (smart young and old people) and resources (wealth and knowledge), but we have a deficit of gifted men and women who are sincere and resolved to lift up the race and humanity at the same time.

In conclusion

Positive Black consciousness has been purged from our collective thinking by many processes (of religion, gang culture, and music) and replaced with a psychology of victimhood. A mentality that perpetuates confusion and frustration. Younger generations have been forced to acknowledge and bear witness to the racial animus and aggression of the empire - in the form of cop killings, killings by rogue white supremacist, and everyday prejudice. The tensions between "us" (Blacks), the State and white public is undeniable. Nevertheless, without a coherent philosophy to organize their frustration and energy around our people are left with nothing but 45 million different opinions and feelings of hopelessness. Therefore it is imperative that our young people be given a narrative that will bind them together. Not as a mass of victims born on a plantation a long time ago; but as modern people who must seize power, and embrace responsibility. Those who want to do gods work must present a narrative that will bind people together while recognizing and respecting their ethnic, religious, and political difference.

# SECTION IV

# THE MOYNIHAN REPORT 1965

# ONE OF MANY WARNINGS

The United States is approaching a new crisis in race relations. In the decade that began with school desegregation decision of the Supreme Court, and ended with the passage of the Civil rights act of 1964, the demand of Negro Americans for full recognition of their civil right was finally met. The efforts, no matter how savage and brutal, of some State and local governments to thwart the exercise of those rights is doomed. The nation will not put up with it -- least of all the Negroes.

The present moment will pass. In the meantime a new period is beginning. *[a new reorganization of caste structure] In this new period the expectations of the Negro Americans will go beyond civil rights. Being Americans, they will now expect  that in the near future equal opportunities for them as a group will produce roughly equal results, as compared with other groups. This is not going to happen. Nor will it happen for generations  to come unless a new and special effort is made. There are two reasons First the racist virus in the American  blood stream still afflicts us: Negroes will encounter serious personal prejudice for at lest another generation.  Second, three centuries of sometimes unimaginable mistreatment have taken a toll on the Negro people.

(The Patrick Moynihan Report 1965) 1

The Moynihan report is important for several reasons. First, it is a government report wherein the author gives an honest critique of American racial caste system. And Second, the author tackles the psychological, sociological, and organizational fallout from those who have bore the brunt of American style oppression - the Black male and his Family.

Although I use the term 'caste' to describe Black and white past and present social structure, it does not conflict with Moynihan's' findings that: "the racist virus in the American bloodstream still afflicts us: *Negroes will encounter serious personal prejudice for at least another generation.*" Making racism part of America's cultural DNA, and the (White vs. Black) caste structure too durable to fade in a few generations. Moynihan did not underestimate the collective institutional prejudice we would continue to face. I see American culture no different than any other culture that wrestles with caste dilemmas; they never quite go away. Racism is to white America what Jihad is to the Arab world - both reason that when things get confusing or tough: we can resort to our old laws / ways of doing things. The Second conclusion of Moynihan that: *"three centuries of...unimaginable mistreatment has taken a toll on the Negro people"* *represents the next part of this essay.*

## THE BROKEN FAMILY

Many things stick out as I read the Moynihan Report; the first is that it conceals far more than it reveals. This is consistent with government documents whose authors know that reports of such nature would eventually become part of the public record. As with anything said or done by others concerning Blacks I had to assess the credibility of the information and the intention behind the document. I quickly concluded the intention behind the Moynihan report to be sincere. The report truly is meant to send a warning that immediate measures were needed  in order to correct the crimes committed against Blacks or else the country as a whole and Blacks particularly would suffer irreparable injury.

I found the information used to support the report to be credible; insofar that philosophy, history, statistics, social science, and sociology can be utilized to predict the future. The document painted a  grim picture of the Black future by using the past (1865) and present (1965) trajectory of the Black family as a  measure. Fifty something years after the release of the Moynihan report much of the forecasts have borne  out or remained consistent with what Moynihan and others  predicted.

As forecasted,  Black males of the inner city continue to struggle under the weight of history, abuse, isolation, and ignorance. They still experience high levels of unemployment;  escape through drugs, alcohol, and fantasy; they are still growing up without responsible men in the  home and father children which they are not responsible for. These males are responsible for committing high levels of intra group murder and robbery. The Black family cannot be categorized as a "family" at all, but something else (survival units) where women are the leadership, educators and breadwinners. However they too are floundering on many fronts.  Continued dependence on welfare or public assistance is a short term  comfort and long term curse; and Black social  disorganization is a bewildering impediment. In sum, the lowest class of Blacks have been collectively left behind  in the competition  of races and ethnicities.

What Moynihan observed others had long recognized  as inevitable. Fifty years before Moynihan's  report Stemmons wrote: *"...Negroes are turning against society with the reckless desperation born of despair."*2 The Moynihan report  confirms that elements in the United States government had for once recognized that the  plight of Black people is not one of their own making. And that  the "unimaginable" abuse, racism and isolation had in fact altered (for the worst) the  future path of Blacks in America.  The Moynihan report is in five sections or 'chapters.'

Chapter  (I) addresses: "The Negro American Revolution." Which is more or less an overview of the Civil Rights movement with its  grievances, goals, hopes, dreams - and limitations.  The second chapter (II) covers the "Negroes American Family." And documents the social and statistical evidence of the fragility and probable continued decline of the Black Family, as a stable and healthy institution. Also noting that many Black families have risen above their circumstances, and for the most part seem to be on firmer footing; however these represent a minority and it would be a mistake to look at those best situated  and judge all Blacks, because the majority are struggling.

The third chapter (III) tackles: "the Roots of the Problem" beginning with slavery and Reconstruction the report chronicles the American social structure  of isolation, oppression and then urban chaos in which the Black family was forced to evolve; and the price of emasculation (never achieving  manhood) paid particularly by Black males for being a target of state sanctioned violence. The fourth chapter (IV) speaks to the: "Tangle of Pathology." That is, the complex  habits, customs, and beliefs,  prevalent in urban  settings that "retard their progress" and act as self-inflicted wounds for each generation.

The first 'pathology' and one that got much attention was the weak family structure resulting from a matriarchal system of family organization (female dominated  households). This domination of Black women which extends out into education and the labor force, according to Moynihan, is considered a disadvantage in a patriarchal (male dominated) society; because ultimately the Black male is less influential (relative to other males in society and compared to his own woman) and thus has no real stake in maintaining family or social cohesion. This  along with chronic unemployment inevitably causes the Black male to retreat from responsible family life. This in turn leads to all the anti-social behavior associated with self-hate, crime, and escape into fantasy, drugs, and alcohol. Resulting in  children without fathers which is the source of  social decay. The next pathology Moynihan named was "Delinquency and Crime." Particularly the epidemic of violence and unorganized crime.  The third pathology was "Alienation" or the "turning against society" by retreating into a subculture where unemployment, drug abuse, amoral, and immoral behavior is normal.

The fifth chapter (V) and shortest, pertains to: "The case for National Action." Which is a call for responsible people in governmental position to do  something rather than nothing to help the Negro and his Family. The report makes a few interesting points, for instance, Moynihan notes there are "many persons" both within and [outside] the government who "do not feel that a problem exist." Or, that "matters will take care of themselves in the normal course of events." He also noted, there is a view "held by a number of responsible persons,  that this problem may in fact be out of control." It is here - in the last section - that I have found the one line that is the most profound. And  in my opinion causes the greatest confusion and divide between Black people as a group, Black people and others, and even divides individual Blacks in their own  soul.  Moynihan concludes: *"At this point, the present tangle  of pathology is capable of perpetuating itself without assistance from the white world. The cycle can be broken only if these distortions  are set right."*

## NO ONE IS COMING TO SAVE US

The sooner we understand this basic fact the sooner we can get busy doing the important work of healing and building. These "distortions" will not be "set right" by any government intervention that does not have us manning the ship. The "unimaginable" abuses we have suffered, that have set us on this course, no longer matter. Apart from the comprehension of our current  predicament our past victimization does not factor into the equation of our reorganization and rehabilitation.  Our problems are ours to figure out and resolve; we need not remind white people "what they did to us" they already know. Some  of them know better than us. The ones who care so be it, the ones who could care less, so be it. We can / must utilize the mechanism of the State in our journey out of hell and in our path to power. However, we cannot rely on the state to do something for us while we sit back  praying for a good outcome. That includes: teaching our children their ABCs, the difference between right or wrong; and  cleaning up the drug  infested neighborhoods - house by house, and  block by block.

## SELF DESTRUCTION/ AND BLACK

## INTELLECTUAL DENIAL

"Self-Destruction" was the title of a popular 1988 song by an all-star cast of rappers. "Self-destruction, we're headed  for self-destruction," was  the chorus line throughout the song. The central theme of the rappers was that Black people are 'self-destructing' by their behavior and personal views. It was a clear critique of urban crime and criminals. It did  not skirt the issues: drug dealers, robbers, and gang bangers were directly addressed and their behavior singled out for being  detrimental  against the community. "I never ever ran from the Klu Klux Klan  and I shouldn't have to run from a Black man," said Kool Mo Dee.

In the 1980s and 1990s this rap song was not strange in its subject matter; many rappers were critical of the criminal lifestyle and these rappers were credible and iconic within a burgeoning culture. Even rappers who lambasted  the welfare system as bad  and welfare recipients as lazy, (Just-ice "Welfare Recipient"/ The Desolate One).3  This tradition is still present in the hip hop but is relegated to the underground conscious rap. Those of a certain age remember the criticism of Black leaders over the issue of gangsterism being introduced into the mainstream culture  in the early 1980s-90s. The lyrics of Tupac were  criticized, and in his song (How Do you  want it?) he attacked  African American Congress woman Deloris Tucker. Ice Cube and  many other rappers also addressed the Black critics of gangsta rap. African American leaders were called "Uncle Toms" and many other names.

Unlike to 1980s and early 1990s gangsta rap is no longer a marginal genre  within the culture of hip hop. It is the core of the culture. Today many if not most mainstream rappers claim to either be criminals (drug dealing  murderers); or to be associated with criminals  (making them criminal by association).  Open affiliation with gangs is almost mandatory for street credibility within the rap culture. I believe today that a song like 'Self Destruction' would be hard to make. There has been such a shift within Black culture that it is no longer capable of self-criticism. This change has also happened in the Black intellectual tradition.

As I read literature that spans over a hundred years I  find many Black  leaders and authors who were unafraid to place responsibility of Black behavior squarely at the feet of Black people. Whether it be Booker T. Washington,  Garvey, Woodson, Du Bois, Elijah Muhammad, Malcolm X, Farrakhan,  N. Akbar, Francis Cress, Amos Wilson, the list is truly long.  Many of our early most cherished leaders  would be labeled  as "conservatives" and accused of "blaming the victim" by the  current Black intelligencia. The same would be said of many early rappers. Today no one can speak ill of people who engage in all manner of self-destructive actions. Nothing can be said about Black  males not taking care of their children; or reckless promiscuity of the youth. The murders, killings and general celebration of death by segments of the culture is also off limits. Some go so far as to deny the killings are even happening by claiming that 'the statistics are off.'  No one can say anything about teens using abortion as  birth control. No one (Black or white) can say anything about any of it; they can only think it, see it, and know it. They are not allowed to name it. How did we get here?  I have two theories.

<u>First</u>, Black America is reeling from the fallout of four decades of the crack epidemic, AIDS, gun violence,  and mass incarceration. These have decimated entire  families, communities and neighborhoods. Because of this we are understandably defensive when it comes to the State targeting  our youth  for punishment. <u>Secondly</u>, the obstacles we face as a people are so enormous that instead of attacking the "pathologies" that plague us, we have turned

away from them and set our eyes on abstract foes and elusive targets. We call them: the Prison Industrial Complex, Republicans, privatization, budget cuts, charter schools, white people. We must answer these questions for ourselves: are we are trying to escape our central (pathological) problems by conflating them with larger problems? It is easier to demonize an abstraction like 'the government' instead of doing the hard work of nation-building? Are we avoiding personal (individual & collective) responsibility by blaming only the system? Are we afraid of sacrifice, and fearless action? Are we our own worst enemies? Are we helpless? Do we wait for the government to fix everything? Where does our responsibility end and the government's begin? Are we only victims and not human beings endowed with agency and power? Who is to blame for making us feel so helpless?

Fifty years after the Moynihan report author Ta Nehisi Coates was tasked with writing an anniversary article examining the "*Black Family in the age of mass incarceration.*" It was marketed as a response to the Moynihan report but fifty years after the fact. 4 It was not about the Black Family whose real and complex problems got little attention, as Coates focused first on the Patrick Moynihan childhood, psychoanalysis, and legacy. Secondly Coates attention was aimed at crime data and the prison industrial complex or as he calls them: "grey wastes of our carceral state." He describes decades of crime statistics, patterns and even international trends. Coates is particularly focused on the prison system. It is not until page 15 of his article that the 'Black family' is first mentioned; in my view most of his data held little relevance.

Coates says, the "carceral state has had far reaching consequences for the economic viability of Black families." Apart from some intellectual gibberish about employment data he says nothing that a human can relate to. He briefly discusses the effects of incarceration of Black males on their families and children. Then cites a National Research Council report claiming that: "more than half of fathers in state prison report being the primary breadwinner in the family." A statement I find to be laughable. I would estimate that same percentage were actually some type of addict, who lived either wholly or partly dependent on women. And existed as nomads fending for themselves only. Coates is beginning to paint his picture of the helpless Black male criminal/ ex-prisoner whose family is saddled with the burden of his absence and even his re-entry into society.

Coates third section delves into his trip to Michigan to visit a woman and former crack addict who had done 18 years in prison for murder; he also interviewed a man who had done time. Coates provides accurate but general information about doing time and re-entering society. Page 23 of Coate's report reveals itself to be an article on the general effects and consequences of incarceration upon criminals.

Section four of Coates article predictably recounts the past victimization of Black people. Similar to chapter III of Moynihan's report entitled: "The roots of the problem" which provides a brief history of Black oppression at the hands of the State and white civilians. Coates provides a litany of Black injustice spanning more than a century. He catalogues how Blacks were singled out and victimized and villainized to justify our oppression. On page 35 Coates says: "It is patently true that Black communities, home to a class of people regularly discriminated against and impoverished, have long suffered higher crime rates." Again the Black family is missing from this section and instead an overview of general Black suffering is offered.

Section five of the article is similar to section four; Coates references the historic demonization of Blacks by former Congressman and social scientist. He shows how former White House insiders admitted that crime was used as a political tool to undermine and attack Black organization during the Nixon administration. He touches on the posture of both parties when it came to crime and the harmful reactive policies written into law. He blames the Democrats and Republicans for sponsoring crime bills detrimental to Blacks. Specifically he cites laws that imposed mandatory-minimum sentences -  that determined the length of time prisoners  had to serve or the type of terms judges could hand out. Coates focuses on the language of journalist, social scientist and even Blacks that cast a "dark" and ominous aura over the future of the Black male and his environment.

He even  castigates Moynihan for seeming to partake in this demonization. Coates says that "many African Americans concurred that crime was a problem," and he cites Jessie Jackson commenting on his fear of Black males. Coates says of Jackson: "he was speaking of a  very real fear of violent crime that dogs Black communities." Then he plunges head long into  linguistic gymnastics with the following statement: "*The argument that high crime is  the predictable result of a series of  oppressive racist policies_does not render the victims of those policies bulletproof. Likewise, noting that fear of crime is well grounded does not  make that fear a solid foundation for public policy.*"  [Why does Coates place it in such enigmatic phraseology? /intellectual mumbling ]

The rest of  section five  shows that so called liberals were complicit in creating new laws that supported the growth of the prison industry. Which was a way to boost employment for whites. He  goes on to say the "Dark predictions of rising crime did not bear out." [in other words the crime was overblown all hype] He ends this section by saying that it was all just a ploy for political gain. The Black "super-predator" criminal class that was predicted to rise by many sociologist was the stuff of fantasy. He quotes Bill Clinton making a volte-face about the success of his own 1994 Crime bill. Coates forgets to mention that prior to the  "Clinton Crime Bill" Black politicians and community leaders had been advancing their own "tough on crime" legislation for two decades. And  themselves supported the 1994 legislation. See, *Locking Up our Own, Crime and Punishment in Black America,* by James Forman Jr. Again the Black family is absent in the discussion Coates is busy excoriating his liberal friends  about their sins.

Section six of Coates' article features a few Black families; one family's son (Odell) has been incarcerated for 41 years. The crux of the section is to demonstrate the difficulties a family faces when they have a loved one behind bars. Again, it documents the evolution in some aspects of criminal law - parole and sentencing. The article talks briefly about Odell's health as he has contracted hepatitis. It mentions the financial and emotional cost families bare. And that Odell, in all likelihood, suffered from childhood lead poisoning. Briefly Coates mentions "lifers" and their difficulty obtaining parole. Coates pivots to environmental factors, specifically housing, and zoning laws that were responsible for locking Blacks into the slums of America.

In section seven Coates then heads to Detroit where he spent time with a community activist and sociologist; who seem to vindicate Moynihan in their description of how their society decayed right before their eyes. They drove around the old neighborhood and recalled the good old days when segregated Black folk had businesses of their own. A time prior to "[t]he Community collapsed, and [the] value system became surviving versus living. [Before] drugs, gangs, lack of education all came to the forefront." One of the men who came of age in the 1970s and 80s describes how even back then most of the children he was raised around had fathers who had been to prison and mothers who were dead. At the end there is nothing new of substance that has not been discussed ad infinitum by both Black and white authors. Up until now the article has been nothing but a compacted version of Michelle Alexander's book *'The New Jim Crow colorblindness in the age of Mass incarceration.'*

In section eight after casting doubt on Moynihan's predictions throughout the article Coates is forced to concede: "*A raft of sociological research has indeed borne out Moynihan's skepticism about the future of Black progress as well as his warnings* [about the direction of the family and Black male.]" Since Coates cannot impeach Moynihan with lack of sincerity and incompetence he plays the sexist card. The Moynihan report "is flawed because it is a fundamentally sexist document." That promotes not just family but a patriarchal structure of family. Revealing how desperate Coates is not to discuss what the "raft of sociological research has borne." Furthermore if Coates believes in what he wrote then he should know that his catalog of evidence constituted proof of war against Blacks. And that his introduction of "reparations" or "damages" into the discussion is an exercise in futility.

At this point I find it unnecessary to go any further, Coates' article is not about "the Black Family." It is another victim narrative written for white liberals so that they may pity Blacks. It addresses in no substantive manner the struggle that we face, it has no plan of action for Black people because it was not written for us. Why would Coates concern himself with Moynihan when plenty of Blacks had made the same predictions? And even advocated for the same "patriarchy" style of family structure. The type of two parent home Coates himself was raised in and benefited from. The same domestic arrangement that made Coates himself into well-adjusted person despite being in a city where young males die young. Why would Coates dodge the ravages of drugs, disease, and crime that plague Black families? Why does Coates paint such a dismal pessimistic future of the gray wastes and carceral state without discussing the actual complexities of crime and prison?

## OUR PROBLEMS AND THE SOLUTIONS ARE BEYOND GOOD AND EVIL

Yes, it is true that mass incarceration is a problem. It is also true that our men and women are overcharged and receive bad representation by their attorneys. It is also true that many sentences are draconian and unjust. It is also true that too many innocent men are languishing in prison; and the justice system is equally as ruthless and remorseless in the way it administrates the law over our people. It is also true that in prison men are turned into zombies by forced psychotropic medications; it is also true that in prison there is inferior medical treatment and as a result prisoners die. It is also true that inmates are kept pacified through the use of strategic coercion, violence and brute force.  It is also true that in most prisons the ignorance of prisoners is manufactured and preferred. It is also true that incarceration breaks down family contact and makes it difficult to maintain bonds. It is also true that drug culture (starting with alcohol) begat our violent culture,  which in turn, gave rise to our current prison culture.

However, it also true that prison protects society because it houses (sadistic, cruel, wicked and extremely violent) people who cannot otherwise function in civil society, and must be removed with force. How do we stop people from committing violence without removing them from our mist either permanently or for a predetermined period of time? Some people are able to benefit from this forced banishment and thrive.  If a person  has improved themselves during their time in confinement it becomes obvious to himself and others. On the other hand, it appears that prison may make some worst. There is no way to know if prison made a person worse, or  simply quarantined someone in moral decline. I believe the conditions of confinement are the most important determinant of personal progress and mental health.

It is also true  prison inadvertently saves lives by snatching men and women off the streets, forcing them out of addiction.  Prison does what no family intervention or drug treatment could have accomplished. The grip of  addiction is so powerful that without prison many would never be able to stop smoking, shooting up, snorting or popping their poison of choice until the angel of death called them back.  Likewise, they would never have stopped committing the crimes that it takes to supply their habits and their lives would become more depraved at every attempt to feed their addiction. Prison effectively stops the addict in their tracks, saving them from themselves and often saving the neighborhood and the addict's family from their self-induced madness.

In this sense - for the addict, community, and family - prison acts as a brief respite from the devil's grip. If not for prison every person they robbed, pointed a gun at, home invaded, old person beat, woman raped, every trick they pulled, every family member swindled, or every act of child neglect would multiply without end. There is no stopping someone whose drug cravings assume control over their instincts, and personality.  It is quite common knowledge among prisoners that the families of many incarcerated people prefer them to be there.  'At least I know where you are at (so I can stop worrying about you being dead),' mothers tell their children. It is the best way to communicate to your child, 'you're better off in there for now.'  For many people not even prison can stop their addition. As this is being written a new generation of inmates have discovered mind altering chemicals that have a profound effect on their mental health. They are pursuing these drugs at their own peril;  prisoners are now having psychotic episodes with increasing frequency. No one except  the creators of these liquid-based hallucinogenic drugs knows what they contain.

Prison has many down sides because it houses a collection of those considered mentally ill, violent, fools, or geniuses. It is a melting pot of: the young and old, the amoral and the immoral, the cruel and the kind, the saints and satans.  Prisoners housed in maximum security facilities are particularly aware of the human depravity spectrum. It is common the hear people comment: 'If I see that guy on my street around my children I have to kill him.' If there were no prisons we would have to institute a firing squad in every city or county. There are some very sick people in this world there's no other way around it.

I take issue with those who complain  of "mass incarceration, the prison industrial complex, grey wastes, and carceral state," but have no solutions. I know for a fact that most of them have no idea what is going on behind prison walls.  Their information is always  cookie cutter, they cannot propose effective legislative or policy changes to reform Black neighborhoods or prisons  because they really have no understanding of the nature of the beast.  They know sociology and statistics but do not understand people. Their gaze is intellectual even if it is heartfelt. They are not even honest in their critique, they are only here to paint the bleakest picture of reality and the most abstract solutions to the problems.

Their writings and statements are even more pessimistic than prisoners or people from the so called "grey wastes" themselves. All of my friends are former criminals or current criminals, and if I talked about their reality in the grim terms that  Coates does they would think that I had lost my mind. Men and women are in prison writing books, taking courses and classes, learning trades, creating art, playing the stock market,  studying business, starting businesses, learning/ practicing law, studying philosophy and planning their future. Some are even  pretending to repent. Hustlers are by their nature dreamers and optimistic people.  They see the bright side of (their own) life because they have to. Prison is partly what you make it, likewise reentry is partly what you make it. Those who cannot stop using drugs, and alcohol or blame  others for everything that goes wrong have a difficult time in prison and outside. If you cannot refrain from pills, drug, and drink you are unlikely maintain employment. If you have a  gambling addiction the chances of saving money is slim.  Those who have not  reached emotional maturity  are doomed to a life of conflict and weak family ties; they will never maintain stable relationships. Those who live by deception and animal instinct are only at ease around their victims. In truth some of these men are given chance after chance for decades. Many get vocational training, and schooling only to squander it when they get home.

Furthermore, unlike white liberals, who will put their money and time where their mouth is, few Blacks are spearheading movements to get into prisons to help transform the hearts and minds of violent gangsters or to make contact with the unfortunate. They would rather believe that "super thugs" don't exist and are boogymen invented by Bill and Hillary Clinton. The Department of Corrections of any state needs secrecy, brutality and mystery to operate because much of its behavior is corrupt and illegal. Therefore, prison administrators and corrections personnel hate liberals; because they are the only people ready to engage prisoners no matter their level of education or nature of their crime. Liberals are always ready to interact  with prisoners themselves. They come as teachers, academics and  (as much as they can) as equals.  They don't want to just pass laws they want to see and hear from the people themselves. My only issue with liberals is their infatuation with the victim narrative. And their inability to speak to the soul. Prisoners don't need to be told 'the system is evil.' They need to be told 'the system has corrupted you, now what are you going to do about it?'

If they had any sense, Black aid groups and organizations would be beating the doors down and trying to get into prison to reform the men and women. These are same men and women who will return  to urban neighborhoods, and the same men and women with street credibility that can change the culture from the inside. In prison there is a captive audience starving for new ideas and points of view. They want to be stimulated, engaged, and are open to criticism and self-reflection. It is the perfect time  to get through to them. Yet most Black volunteers come as proselytizers of religion and have nothing else to offer. Blacks will propose well-meaning legislation from afar, but getting their hands dirty and getting to the heart of the problem they cannot do. Criminal-minded male or female must hear from the people concerned about them.  They must be told directly how they matter, in addition to how their negative behavior effects their families, neighbors, and strangers. They will not be wished away or denounced out of existence by angry panels. Prison and prisoners can only be engaged, confronted and reformed by people honest enough to admit that human problems are beyond good and evil.

## THEY DON'T WANT TO TALK ABOUT THE "PATHOLOGIES"

I have no problem with Coates personally. I have heard him speak and discuss his books. I've had my eye on him since he came on the scene. He has a likable but melancholy personality. I have not read any of his books and take no position with respect to them, although they sound interesting in subject matter. I have a problem with this genre of literature which enumerates a litany of Black suffering, but makes the Black male appear helpless and free of fault. They paint a picture in which Blacks have no agency whatsoever. I know these stories are written for an white academic audience, but nonetheless they end up in our mouths as talking points. Black people are being trained to think only about their limitations and victimization; but never about their role in their own demise and the power they have over destiny.

Coates (and those like him) have nothing to offer as a plan of action for the Black people. His intellectual prowess is not going to be put to use on the ground. They are not going to be in the trenches guiding those they write about. The people need and want a modern day Marcus Garvey, Elijah Muhammad, and Malcolm X. They are not looking for a James Baldwin who will write about Negro misery from a chateau in Europe. I fear that young minds eager for action will approach this victim literature for life's answers but only find a diatribe against the government and white people. Black people want someone to give them hope and show them the way. They are in search of leadership. They want to be led out of these grey waste and are ready to proceed 'by any means necessary.' However, they will be unfulfilled because Black intellectuals have no answers except to say: 'the government did this to you and they need to fix it.'

Let us be honest, Coates and his kind do not know what to do with common drug addicts; let alone an army of testosterone filled drug addicts with machine guns. He does not know what to do with a teenage murderer drunk off the celebrity of his infamy, who finds his purpose in a rising body count. He does not know what to do with the man who gets five years for murder, and is released, then commits another murder. He does not have a plan for snaking lines of addicts that span entire city blocks. And he has no solution for the children whom must maneuver these lines to get to and from school. He does not have instructions for fifteen year old mothers addicted to PCP, heroin or crack, or for prisoners entering or emerging from prison. He does not know what to tell a single mother heading a household what to do with her son whom she has given everything to, but for some  reason has turned to the streets. He has no plan for systematically clearing  drug infested areas of its worst elements. Or what to do about the gang leader with two hundred  men under his command and leaving prison with delusions of grandeur. He does not know how to comprehend the Black male who does not fit his victim narrative; who had good parents and a good home and schooling, but was infatuated with the criminal lifestyle and the desire to be "thugged out."

He has never sat around a council of gang leaders while they discuss the jurisprudence of killing women and children, and come to a consensus that they "must evolve" with the times and so killing even innocent children is acceptable.  He does not know what to do with violent men for whom Black life - man, woman or child - means nothing. He does not know what it is to see men who have done nothing except kill women or children come to prison and be welcomed as heroes. Has he seen men with five and six murders laugh and joke about "never missing" and complain that the courts did not give them "due process?"

All these types are already present in the community or pray to be released back into  communities so they can finish the whirlwind of chaos they started. Has Coates seen the males who come to the "gray wastes" he calls prisons and spend thousands of dollars of their family wealth (proudly) and never buy one reading book. What are they saying about the massive transfer of family wealth taking place  through the criminal justice  system. Families are not paying college tuitions, endowing  institutions, supporting charities, or putting equity into their homes; they are paying for lawyers, fines, fees, prison commissary - for decades! He has no solutions so he does not talk about it. He does not talk about it therefore he will never have credibility.

The simple fact is government cannot and will not save us from ourselves. Those who harp about past and present state crimes against Blacks fail to realize that we are on our own. Many of our problems transcend anything beyond the government's power to fix. The state is not going to micro manage regressive cultural traits that give us a disadvantage in the modern world.  I have been in prison for over two decades and I can say with  certainty that many of problems I observe men and women suffering from cannot be remedied by the government intervention. My problem with many writers (particularly from the left) is that  they want to discuss the pathologies  plaguing the Black community. But instead of confronting the issue head on  they divert our attention  to the perceived origins of those problems. Instead of addressing the mentalities that create urban murder rates, addictions,  or broken homes they discuss the victimization of  Blacks in order to explain why we are in such shambles. Instead of coming down to the ground level in order  to solve these problems. They point to the government and guilt people into handing more money over. As long as the government is always to blame then nobody will confront the issues and wrestle with complex problems. We as a community  or as individuals are never  forced to confront what we have become or who we are.

The old tradition of self-criticism and striving toward collective refinement is gone. Garvey, Elijah Muhammad, and Malcolm X came to 'wake the dead.' They understood our people were in a profoundly underdeveloped state, and it was this state they, (and the rest of our leaders) came to address. Our leaders were resurrecting our dead minds and correcting our backward behavior. Now nobody wants to wake the dead they want to give lectures about the killers and their crimes. No one will confront the Black male about his thinking because he is a baby that must be protected. However, it is well understood that no group with such institutionalized instability in its family structures, will ever produce healthy communities or individuals. Deep down everyone knows we will never get our act together, because our real concerns are not being addressed. Until there is a reorganization of the  Black mind, community and body politic- our path is set, and it is will not be a good outcome for a majority  of us. They can throw all the  money at schools they want, changes all of the crime laws they want, create all the reentry programs they want. This will never divert our present course. These are Herculean obstacles for us to overcome, nevertheless, we have to face them head on. We cannot be afraid to discuss them openly

I have been through the criminal justice system most of my life and the people I have encountered need much more than a history lesson. There men  and women who have such deep psychological or emotional problems that nothing but a stern, empathetic,  and loving community can save them. Men and women are in effect dealing with  adolescent developmental challenges throughout their entire adult lives. In many cases, traumatized and damaged people are infecting their children with personality disorders. The type of behavioral patterns that stand in the way of the formation of healthy human relationships. We are producing generations of  children and adults who are inheriting personality traits that make it difficult to distinguish them from truly mentally ill  persons.

The state is not designed to reach deep into the human soul or mind and fix the things that are broken within us. Only men and women who are willing to tell the truth can do this work. We need leaders on the ground and on the front line, not (ivory tower) sociologist, psychologist, historians, lecturers, or intellectuals. These are people best suited for consultation in government policy planning or decision making processes. Black  people need prophets, messengers, and friends of god who will bring them a new law, and demand that  traditions of morality  be obeyed. People who will live among them and guide them out of the darkness and demand that they turn away from their slide toward anarchy. Men and women from among them who can criticize the culture for its decadence and hedonism. Men and women who will teach them how to strive for perfection in this life. Most importantly men who are willing to go to war with enemies within the culture in order to save it from itself. We need apostles who do not fear rebuke, poverty, punishment, or death!

The goal of the leader is to establish a culture and society in which the most intellectually and spiritually refined human beings are being produced as a matter of normal standard tradition. The leader must show people the way by example. He or she must establish the institutions that will make this cultural transformation possible and permanent. The leader will not be doing the work the people who are to be resurrected will be building this new society themselves; this is the only way they will cherish what they have created. The leader is there to lay down the law and the logic. He or she is there to write the constitution and show them how it works in practice. The leader must show the people  how to choose leaders from among themselves and what these leaders must act like. The leader must then warn the people of what to fear and not to stray and then he or she must die and leave the people to fend for themselves.

The government cannot make men love and take care of their children.

The government cannot make men stop drinking their lives away.

The government cannot stop men from using drugs.

The government cannot make men save money

The government  cannot stop men from gambling their money away.

The government  cannot stop men spending their money on things they can't afford.

The government  cannot make men enjoy work.

The government cannot prevent men from loving the street life.

The state cannot remove the desire to kill from the heart.

The state cannot stop men from wanting to be drug dealers.

The state cannot show men how to buy land instead of sneakers.

The government cannot make man settle down with a woman and raise a family.

When I say "the government," I mean the current type of government we have. The American constitution affords many liberties in this country. We do not live in a socialist paradise. The State has limited jurisdiction in most personal matters. We have to come to terms with the arrangement we have  as it pertains to the individual power versus the State. These are problems that we must fix on our own. Unlike China who can solve such things with an edict we are force to be masters of our own fate.

*******

Blacks are not forced to live in the rat and trash infested slums of the early 20th century or of thirty or forty years ago, nor are they trapped because of housing covenants. They are not legally restricted in their national and international movement. Neither are they locked out of information as was possible twenty five years go. The availability and ubiquitousness of military grade weaponry ensures  we are not helplessly vulnerable to white terrorism or State violence; however, there is still a pervasive victim mentality just beneath the surface of the Black psyche.

"I would blame my environment but ain't no reason why I be buying expensive chains."

Jay Z

I believe many Blacks (more than is usually represented in the media - Black conservatives not included) believe that the problems that we have are at this current point more self-inflicted than  we care to  admit. <u>This is not to say that the white majority has ever or will ever cease to try and  maintain their political and economic superiority by using  laws, policy, and economic sabotage in order to maintain distance. This  not to say that we are on an "equal" footing as  compared with other groups who have not gone through what we have in the last one hundred and fifty years</u>. This is

230

to say that too many of us are not putting our best foot forward, and have settled for an inferior caste status within the empire. I do believe many Blacks have abandoned ideas of striving toward collective advancement as well as personal refinement.

The fact remains that there is a tremendous amount of latitude to operate within and outside of the U.S. And there are ways and means at our disposal (social, political, material, and other) to thwart, neutralize, and counter further aggression from whites, Asians, or hostile Latinos. We are far better positioned to excel economically, socially, and politically than we were 40, 50, or a hundred years ago. Had our ancestors, who trekked out of the south a hundred years ago, been met by the social problems we face they would size up the obstacles and dismiss them as nothing.

The person who has not become numb by the constant drip of misery must take inventory of the family, and friends lost from drugs, disease, and violence. The decimation of Black families, one person at a time, must alarm those not emotionally dead. I asked myself: 'what would I do to stop the slow carnage that is mass incarceration, violence, generational ignorance, addiction, and prostitution; where men are reduced to killing each other and informing or lying on one another for survival, and women stoop to unspeakable actions for money? Where child neglect begins in utero and children exist as burdens to their family. The answer is, I would do anything, spare no corner, no hallway, no block, no person, no man, or woman! In order to eradicate what has proven to be a culture of death we may have to ignore the law, mercy, and grace! When cancer is eating the body and spreading to other parts it must be cut out, burned, and radiated just to save to the whole.

If we want to reach a higher level of existence we must confront some serious questions. Black people must ask themselves 'what price are they willing to pay in order to save their body?' We are not used to hard questions, therefore too many so called 'thought leaders' get away with literary babble, when death is at hand. They speak in generalities and abstractions "mass incarceration" "Gray waste." However, they will never articulate what Blacks themselves can do to alleviate or reverse our self-destructive condition. They will storm Capital Hill en masse and make a 'case for reparations' because its sounds radical. They have Blacks believing a government check (or undefined help) will fix four decades of addiction, five decades of government dependence, six decades of family decline, more than a century of mis-education and four centuries of fear. They are lying, and they know it. They have no big ideas only big resentments and little goals.

Coates criticized Moynihan for saying: Black males led "wasted lives." I can personally attest to knowing hundreds of men who are dead from murder. After murder I could count disease, addiction, and stupidity as the leading cause of Black male death. What about those who have gone insane from street life and drug abuse, or those, in prison psychiatric units, lobotomized by state administered medication? I know hundreds of men who were dead before thirty or who never made it to fifty. Women are also suffering from similar fates, however their decline is more debasing and humiliating. I know so many dead that I refuse to count them; I only see them in my dreams from time to time. If you don't want to cry over what's happening it is because you cannot see, refuse look, or mastered the art of compartmentalizing our collective sorrow. Some have resorted to disassociation as a coping mechanism; in order to function they force themselves to block out the idea that a 'we' actually exists.

What is happening in our neighborhoods is so disgusting, criminal, and evil that most dare not look at it. They avert their eyes away from a critical segment of our culture who are on self-destructive autopilot. This is what Moynihan meant when he said: *"At this point, the present tangle of pathology is capable of perpetuating itself without assistance from the white world. The cycle can be broken only if these distortions are set right."* It is also what Francis Cress Welsing meant when [discussing teenage motherhood/ young women rising children alone] wrote:

*The emotional and psychological underdevelopment of an entire people <u>can become chronic and permanent once this dynamic effects a sufficient percentage of the population.</u> As I have previously stated 25% of Black children being born in the U.S. are part of this cycle of emotional underdevelopment - the basis for functional inferiority. Blacks would be horrified if anyone suggested the outright slaughtering of 25% or more of Black children. Again, Blacks scream genocide when outspoken white supremacist suggest sterilization of 25% or more or the Black population. Yet, the aforementioned pattern of child-parent rearing, presently widespread in the Black population, achieves exactly the same results. The only difference is that with Black child-parents, the Black child's death is more painful and drawn out - a living death. It is a living death in a highly complex society to be left unable to sit still in school and achieve academically because of incorrect socialization. It is a living death for a child to be shifted repeatedly from one foster home to another. It is a living death for a child to walk the streets addicted to drugs or alcohol. It is a living death to be a school drop-out. It is a living death to walk the streets as a prostitute. It is a living death to sneak around the streets as a thief. It is a living death to suffer the depression of unemployment because you are uneducated and unskilled.... It is a living death for a child to be confined to a psychiatric hospital. It is a living death to spend a lifetime locked up behind the bars of a juvenile detention center or prison cell....many of these syndromes of living death lead to forms of actual death such as suicide, drug overdose and homicide. More often than not these deaths are the direct result of children raising children. All of the above are related directly and indirectly to the dynamic of white supremacy, which necessitates Black functional inferiority. However, <u>many of the above patterns of living death can be controlled, countered and combated effectively only if the Black community - the entire Black collective - is determined to re-program its individual and collective knowledge, understanding and behavior...</u>*

It is true that we have many residual problems from previous generations; however, there has to be some recognition that many of the problems Blacks face can be controlled because they are largely cultural problems, that have to do with the regulation of group behavior and personal organization. Since all behavior begins at the level of family it is the structure of family that requires the first overhaul. If we ignore this current window of opportunity we will pay for it in the future with the type of loss of life that only third world people recognize.

# SECTION V

# THE SOURCE OF ALL POWER

# FAMILY IS THE FIRST LEVEL OF

# SELF ORGANIZATION IN A

# COMMUNITY

*The cornerstone of the Roman social structure was the household (familia). The State was an association of households, and it was the individual's place in a household that determined his status in the community.*6

This book has been about history, but what is history? History is not only the story of empires, nations, States, great men, and  great women. History is not simply tales of wars, famines, achievements, discoveries, and destruction of  people. History is and will always be first and foremost the story of families. There is a reason that the history, lore, and myths  of  all people - whether it be about their gods,  origin, land, or race - begin with the story of a family.

According to the Egyptian creation myth, in the beginning, only the ocean existed. Then Ra the sun came out of an egg (or flower)... Ra brought forth four children... The Gods Shu and Geb the Goddesses Tefnut and Nut.. Geb (now earth) and Nut (now sky)  had two sons Set and Osiris and two daughters, Isis and Nephthys...[later Osiris and his  sister (now wife) had a son named Horus] From this myth of creation  comes the conception of the ennead, [or] a group of nine divinities and the triad consisting of father, mother and son.7 The early Japanese wove mythological stories to explain the origins of their land. One story says: "[In] a time of the dim distant past,...two gods stood on the Floating Bridge of Heaven. Descending to this island, the gods, one male and one female... conversed in the proper order (the male speaking first), they produced offspring: [which became] the eight main islands."8

I believe nearly four thousand years of resilience of Jewish community and  tradition rest not with their complex laws or customs, but the fact that many of their holy books are  centered around  family life. There is Adam and Eve,  Cain and Abel,  Noah and his children,  Moses and Aaron, David and  Solomon,  Abraham, Isaac, Ishmael, Sarah and Hagar, and  the hundreds of names and families that make the stories in the Bible relatable on a basic human level. They are familiar to us because they are family dramas. The Bible's Proverbs are in fact a father warning and instructing his son in what 'righteousness'  and 'wickedness' are, and how to discern between wisdom and foolishness. The intimate family components of the instruction are the key to their connection with the average man, woman and child. It is  for that reason the Jewish people and traditions have been able to withstand the test of time; and the Jewish holy books are the fountainhead of both  Christianity and Islam.

Christianity begins with a Mary, Joseph, and the birth of an anointed child; Islam begins with Muhammad an orphan raise by his uncle who came into prophethood at age 40 and first converted his wife, household,  and best friend to the new faith. Even the story of the Buddha revolves around a young man sheltered from the reality of life by his family.  By no means did the ancients idealize the family, it was never presented as a perfect arrangement. Osiris was killed by his brother Set, Cain was killed by Abel, and Joseph (Son of Abraham) was betrayed by his jealous brothers. The Buddha's arch-enemy was his cousin. Early in Muhammad's prophethood his arch enemy was his uncle named "Abu Lahab" (father of fire), while at the same time  he was able to continue calling people to Islam because he was protected by his clan or extended family.

The  pattern that emerges in all of these stories is that ancient peoples thought the most important component in deciding the value, fortune, and future of a person was the family; and that an individual's purpose was understood to be determined first by a  healthy relationship with their family. It is clear that  ancient peoples understood that the family was, is, and will remain the most important factor in determining the  health, well-being, and destiny for the individual, community and nation.


## THE INSTITUTION OF FAMILY WAS THE FIRST THING LOST TO PEOPLE PLACED IN BONDAGE AND IT IS THE FIRST THING NEEDED FOR THOSE WHO WANT TO OVERCOME THE EFFECTS OF POWERLESSNESS


*"Even though a large group from the same town had been chosen [in this circumstance], most were left behind: children, husband, wives, brothers and sisters, friends and neighbors... Their journey was a tragic succession of separations...the first severance came between the dead and the living; the second between those who were too old, too weak, too young or too injured to leave and the young and healthy. Along the way, some relatives, friends and neighbors were sold and others died...By the time they walked to the ships, Africans for whom family and community are particularly critical, had already gone through several highly traumatic separations. And the journey was far from over.* 9

The Africans placed in bondage and brought to the Americas were doomed from the start, because  they arrived in the hostile New World without family, and the cocoon of protection it offers. Blacks (certainly in America) did not arrive to the new world as organized family units with mother, father, and children situated neatly on plantations. Africans arrived as individuals sometimes of the same "clan" and what they were allowed to form as familial bonds are concerned were not "families" in the traditional sense of the word - as they understood it or as was understood by their overlords.

FAMILY DEFINED/ By 'family' I do not simply mean men and women who contribute to the genetic composition of a new life, or blood relatives who loosely interact with others they know to be their siblings and kinfolk. I would define family as: People linked by blood, lineage or marriage who are tightly or loosely organized around a division of power, status,  and responsibility. The basis of which is governed by social custom, religious, and civil  law. Families  use marriage and procreation to increase their numbers, acquire power, and transfer power, in addition to perpetuate traditions across generations. Families are biological and social kin units in which every new marriage, birth, and death is accompanied by a prescribed set of rituals and religious rites. My understanding of "family" makes it more of a verb than noun. Family is a continuous action and collective behavior not simply connection based on genetics,  proximity, or static facts. Families are the people who support you and you in return support. Family is something you rely on and contribute to.

*All societies must have a way of replacing their members, and reproduction is essential to the survival of human society as a whole. Within the institution of the family, sexual relations among adults are regulated, people are cared for, children are born and socialized, and newcomers are provided an identity - "a lineage" that gives them a sense of belonging. Just how these activities are carried out varies from society to society, but family, whatever its form, remains the hub of social life in virtually all societies.* 10

Based on what we know about ancient and modern traditional family structure - the way in which Blacks were forced to organize themselves within the American slavery/plantation system did not and could not resemble the complex family structure they were accustomed. The American plantation system like a modern prison sought to obliterate collective identity. The slave had to be individualistic, (even ruthless and cunning) and willing to do anything to save his or her own skin from hunger, whip, rope, chain, fire, sword and bullet.

The slave system (like prison) perfected the manufacture of outwardly docile humans and bred spies, informants, passive, and illiterate persons. Like prison the smart, and rebellious, would be identified and targeted for worse treatment (hated by master and fellow slave), and the crafty individualistic traitor elevated and favored. Under the pressure of this type of setting neither a healthy community or family structure can evolve or exist. Therefore we neither had families nor communities in the strictest sense of the concept.

*"A people with absolutely no memory of their past would be unable to govern themselves successfully, to abide by a proven way of life, and to keep the law; a culture with no traditions, with no memory of past techniques or customs, would be similarly incapacitated.* 11

## OUR 1863-65 EMANCIPATION INTO COMMUNAL ANARCHY

Blacks emerging from slavery (over 4 million) did so without an organic traditional social structure that regulated their behavior when it came to the following areas: procreation, marriage, inheritance, adoption, succession of family authority, and initiation rites for adolescents transitioning into adulthood. Blacks did not have a legal system for enforcing the will of the group or a method of punishing violations of tradition (punishing violators of group law with penalties ranging from banishment to death). These are the sort of basic institutions that governed all people for thousands of years of civilization.

Unlike the Jewish experience who experienced centuries of persecution and being relegated to European ghettos or other forms of segregated oppression, Blacks were not confined on plantations in organized family units. Nor did Blacks possess a three thousand year old religious hierarchy which maintained their own identity, law, order, and literacy. In my view, they did not know how to be family in the most literal sense of the word. How could they when they had no legacy of its communal practice for hundreds of years? Family is the first stage of community government, and without a tradition of self-governing Blacks were emancipated into social anarchy.

I am not suggesting that newly freed slaves did not love each other or have a sophisticated social networks. I am arguing that the agenda of the American slave system was to destroy the African's memory, because brainwashing is a necessary step in the matrix of domination. Generations could not be allowed to transmit and perpetuate the kinship structure of their religious, moral, spiritual, and legal universe, because they would understand who they were and resisted their condition. Of course these people knew they were once "Africans," but what that truly meant was terrorized out of them.

Consequently, African institutions and coping mechanisms never took firm root in collective Black behavior patterns. Those practices that were preserved such as music, ways of worship, individual style, and modes of logic were used in secret or openly as catharsis. I argue that we never had families because the term as we now loosely apply it does not square with the African concept of the term. No one can name any right and obligation - legal, religious, or customary - that any person in bondage ever had over his wife children, parents or siblings in America. Familial organization and rights did not break down during slavery, but were never formed with true substance on American soil - among this class.

The people of blood relations on plantations whether: brother and sister, father and daughter, mother and son, or aunt and uncle did not have legal obligations and rights over one another. They were fungible commodities and could be handled anyway their owners saw fit. There is no doubt that they formed strong life long "family" bonds with each other; bonds that included love, trust and even symbolic or token marriage. However important marriage may have been to them it was nonetheless a ritual ceremony without power in the larger society. This marriage did not even give the male or female any formal authority over their own offspring. There was no legally binding power over property or assets. Actually the modern prisoner has more parental rights than a slave who lived in the same 'home' as his children and wife.

All is not lost, the fact that Blacks still thought it important to observe customs like marriage even when  they knew they were meaningless  (void of legitimacy) outside the slave's context demonstrates a high degree of cultural refinement. Nonetheless, from the following account we get the sense of planning, organization, and control that went into maintaining a traditional African family that was contemporary with our emancipation:

*Cudjo had a happy and active childhood playing with his siblings, climbing trees, and playing the drum. At fourteen he started to train as a soldier by learning how to track, hunt, camp shoot arrows and throw spears. The training lasted several years,...During his adolescence, Cudjo got initiated into Oro, the Yoruba secret male society, which is in charge of controlling and policing society. Some men's duties are to find out and dispose of criminals, accused sorcerers, and witches; to administer justice, and conjure evil for the protection of the village or town. ...Oro holds an annual ceremony during which the initiates meet in the woods for seven to nine days... After which he was offered a  meal with roast meat and palm wine during which he was taught to keep secrets...At nineteen, he was spotted showing interest in a young woman, and his father decided it was time for him to start another phase of initiation...In African cultures that practice it, marriage cannot occur before initiation is completed.* 12

This was the account of Cudjo one of the last slaves bought (illegally) to America in 1858. He and those who arrived with him were captured at the tail end of American slavery which ended in 1863. Cudjo's culture was strange to the American born Blacks, who had lost all memory of these socialization techniques. There are very few slaves or emancipated person in 1863-65 who would have known about or gone through such an elaborate educational process or even understood the concept of freedom in the same way. Cudjo encountered men and women who were domesticated and whose mothers and fathers were domesticated. He lived well into the 20th century and died in 1932. Once free again the small group of Africans chose to self segregate they formed a  community known as 'Africa Town' in Alabama; their descendants are still around and are aware of their own roots. Because these people had not lost the memory of their ways, they saw themselves as distinct from the Blacks who were here - although some did marry native born Blacks. It is said they even had their own laws and  judges.

**********

A Black male remarked to me that: 'he cannot remember one home on his block with a father in the home.' He was from a different town than me but made me think of my own experience. I can recall that only a few homes in my entire neighborhood had men present but many of the men were alcoholics, and drug addicted. Even the Puerto Rican families who generally had more fathers present in the homes suffered from high rates of male  drug and  alcohol addiction. This pattern was already firmly entrenched in the 60, 70s, and 80s. According to sociologist Thomas Wilson, Blacks who migrated to the Northern and Western cities in the beginning of the 20th century (circa 1915) *tended to be more family-stable compared both to those they left behind and those they  encountered  in the north." He says of Black migrants to the north: "They are less likely to bear children outside of marriage and less likely to be divorced or separated from their spouse."13*

242

These weakly established morals soon became meaningless to some of the migrants and certainly to new generations born in the north and not reared under strict religious "morality." In American cities northern Blacks had  been battling the ruthless forces of urban life. It did not take long for the social fabric of the Black world to unravel in a new  setting where victims of quarantine, isolation and discrimination were  crowded together in slums unable to escape their condition. In the north individual behavior was not subject to the authority of (small) rural town traditions; where everyone was some sort of kinfolk or where institutions like the church had real power. By the 1930s (just sixty five  years after slavery) E. Franklin Frazier said of Black migrants in Chicago "the disorganization of Negro life in the city seems at times to be a disease."14  They are still (90 year later) saying the same thing about Black life in Chicago. Furthermore, a hundred years after the great migration it is still known that Black Southern men and women continue to be more family oriented than those in the North. It is well known that Southern men kill other men over their wives or women; whereas such behavior is not considered honorable in  the north.

The same scenario would play out wherever Blacks were concentrated in high numbers under the same conditions. The dark ghettos of America were now in there infancy. By the 1960s (a hundred year after slavery) Moynihan and others were already commenting on the growing prevalence of single mother headed homes; therefore female headed survival units had already taken root in many urban centers.

Hence the destruction of the modern American Black family is multi-layered. First there was the reality of already weak social structures under the strain of white patriarchal aggression. Then the effects of poverty that makes men and women individualistic, desperate and ruthless in their pursuit of objectives. There is manufactured ignorance that functions like a prison, keeping men locked out of power and mobility. There was/ is the exploitation of the poor having to pay higher rents and mortgage prices for inferior living arrangements and  stressing fragile family units.  The hard work of Blacks did not (and does not) reap the same reward  as similarly situated whites or even foreigners. Blacks were also locked out of most of the labor market and  had access to only the lowest wage and least  skilled jobs. There is also the  cold-hard reality of urban life which has always been the center of poverty, illicit activities like drugs, murder, gambling, robbery, prostitution - in other words the epicenters of easy profits.

Before Blacks had arrived in the north en masse most crime and degeneracy was  attributed to the poor "dangerous class" of immigrants who were filling up American cities (Irish then Italians)." 15 In 1880 Charles Loring Brace wrote in "The Causes on Crime": ...an immense proportion of our ignorant  and criminal class are foreign born; and of the dangerous classes here, a very large part, though native-born are of foreign parentage."16 He went on to point out that of the female criminal class many of them were Irish born whereas Irish women at home (Ireland) were  known  to be virtuous. There was much concern for this class. The son's of fragile European family units were helped up, dusted off and turned into American soldiers and a blue-collar work force. They were invested in and subsidized by aid societies, the federal government, and private industry; the goal was to create American 'citizens' from this class, and it largely worked out.  Whereas the discrimination that the Black family (male) had to face  in all its forms doomed an already weakly established institution.

Blacks that were able to escape the cities with their family, morals and sanity intact are better off for it. Everybody in the hood has family from the suburbs who seem to live in a parallel universe. They are hard working people who are  a little naive; for the most part they are well adjusted, attend fair schools, and are non-threatening.  People who generally believe in Christianity and the morality taught by the church. They have their own problems as all people do, but on average they do  not produce multiple generations of the criminal minded,  addicts, or prostitutes. Strong families make for strong neighborhoods and communities.

On the contrary those who remained in urban centers or were trapped by poverty, or socialized complacency have paid a terrible price for it.  Those families (weak, chaotic and fractured survival units) who have remained in urban areas have paid a price in blood, sanity, freedom, health, and progress. They have essentially sacrificed some portion of their families to the principalities of darkness. All families have been touched by early death, disease, murder, prison, gangsterism, and cycles of teenage pregnancy.  The greatest loss has come in the form of sacrifice of successive generations of males to the gods of gangsterism. Black males have succumb to criminal mindedness and have transformed the culture in dangerous ways.

There is no predetermined genetic component to criminality, neither is there anybody who is forced to be a criminal through his or her entire life; this leaves just one thing - culture. Culture helps manufacture the criminal and the criminal helps manufacture culture. Environment influences culture, but culture also influences environment - like wind and temperature both are needed to produce a whirlwind. The evidence points to environmental factors as having  stunted our development - by environmental we mean sustained  economic, intellectual, physical,  and legal attack by a predatory majority. However, because something was true then does not make it true now. Meaning, many of the environmental obstacles that held our ancestors back have been weakened, dissipated, or even vanish. Yet, too many remain stunted in backwards self-defeating behavior. Indeed what I and many others see now is a culture hiding behind the excuse of environment to justify its low expectations and self-destruction.

# POWER AND PROGRESS FOR ALL PEOPLE BEGINS AND ENDS WITH FAMILY

If we are going to  pull ourselves out of the our current condition (individually & collectively) we must first reconstitute the most basic social unit of the family. If we want to reverse the effects of centuries of repression and trauma we must change the way in which the Black male views the institution of  family. As noted by Dr. Cress *"When the Black collective begins to understand that power is directly related not to money but to correct behavior pattern organization, behavior discipline and behavior control on the part  of the individual and the collective, the Black collective will be well on its way towards a new level of political understanding."* 17 Dr. Cress is explaining what seems counterintuitive; that obtaining wealth does not begin with getting actual money but in  the way we organize our daily lives - collective discipline and  behavior.

There is no marching, rioting, protesting, or new Lamborghini, that can change our lives better than the  mundane  life of a father who must educate, feed, and protect his wife and children. I believe there has been a fundamental flaw in our teaching approach as it pertains to the Black male. Let us not fool ourselves, the problems of weak family structure must be laid at the feet of the male. There is no person who is more irresponsible than he. If the male wants to settle down with a wife, is emotionally mature, and has a social  incentive he will do so. Most males do not have a difficult time finding a woman who wants this sort of arrangement and is suited for it. The same cannot be said of women who want to settle down.

If we want Black males to settle down then the exact advantages of forming a family and living a life of responsibility must be conveyed to him while he is still young. I cannot remember anybody explaining to me what I gained from marriage, but I do remember  marriage being depicted as a burden and prison (ball & chain)  for men in the television sitcoms. Marriage is mostly cast as a negative in the media; this is the only impression of marriage that someone unfamiliar with the institution receives.

This is particularly true of males who have not grown up living  in households where this social arrangement is normalized; which now constitutes most of our households.  In essence we want boys to settle down with a wife and to have children, but the advantages of this arrangement are left unsaid. And in the urban centers a stable adult male is so strange that seeing a firsthand example of a solid family unit and its benefits is like seeing a unicorn.

As a solution to this problem I pose that we tell the truth. We must start by teaching our males that 'family' equals power and that the semi-nomadic lifestyles that we have been leading end in weakness and personal impotence. On social media Black nurses in particular have been commenting on the high rate of single Black men in there forties having strokes – and are left without anyone to care for them in their lowest moment. The truth is, American culture is so far from the religious path that 'morality' is ruled out as the starting point of any persuasive argument. Therefore I approach the subject of the importance of family from another angle;  the perspective of power.

At some point the Black male (and female for that matter) must look around (look up) and take special notice of the people who monopolize power. Those people who make the laws that he abides by and those with the  military authority to destroy his soul. He must take stock of the people of wealth who rule the global economy. He must look to the doctors who teach and heal in the greatest medical centers  ever to exist; and take notes from the lawyers he calls when he is in trouble.

The  male must reflect on the habits of world <u>leaders, whatever continent and color they may be</u>. He must ask himself: what do most of these men have in common? If he studies the makeup of the  graduating classes of prestigious universities and see the future leaders of finance,  technology,  and science he will see one thing that most of them share in common. Most of them will have been reared in homes with at least two stable parents, and will themselves go on to enter into this sort of union, as a traditional method of social organization.

In  addition  to  this  their  neighborhoods,  communities, schools, and social clubs will be made up of people who are similarly predisposed to this living arrangement. When these families merge in unions of marriage it is done with the idea that both families will become  stronger  from  this  union  of  blood,  wealth,  status,  and position. And more importantly that the offspring produced within this union will continue the legacy of both lineages and even elevate them by the synthesis of their attributes.  In order to preserve their power and wealth some families resort to marriage  within the family this  is particularly true for Middle-Eastern  cultures. In both Jewish and Arab cultures cousins are wedded without regard for western incest  taboos.

In any event, for those males who have not gotten the memo yet it must be conveyed to them that:  powerful people have customs and  traditions  that  both  leads  them  to  success  and  helps  them maintain  their  power,  position,  and  privilege.  The  formula  for everlasting and perpetual power is that the male must first organize his life around a nuclear family wherein he is the head and leader. This structure  is itself a source of power. Not an energy draining burden as  popularly portrayed. It is the most basic  social  system and  from  it  flows  status,  connections,  credit,   and  privilege.  The benefits of this arrangement is written into law, and is easily observed in every society's institutions. In truth there are many circles that one cannot enter without the mark  of maturity. Marriage says something about the person and their values even before they enter a room and open their mouths. The fact that they have entered into this mutual bond says: *I am stable; I am clear of mind; my value has already been acknowledged by others; I am responsible; I am of this new world but I am still attached to  the old sacred laws;  I can be trusted; I am attached to a larger family;  I am not alone.*

The people who own the actual land, and major industries and even small business in our neighborhoods most likely come from stable family structures. The people we give our money to when we shop for clothes, jewelry and cars come from stable families. People wonder how others can come to America 'alone,' and ignorant of the language and customs, but somehow surpass others who were  born here; what is the secret? The secret is that they are not working for themselves but for something larger. Most people that  come here are not motivated by individualistic goals they come with their family as the constant source of motivation. It is not only their own lives they want to change, but the destiny of their entire family.

Instead of watching the wealth and material possessions of others with the envy of a robber, we need to envy their living arrangements and social structure. The key to power stares us right in the face but we cannot see because we are distracted by materialism. Like children who mistakes  symbols for substance and a mirage for water. The  Black male seeks shiny objects, he looks at the Maserati or Bentley and thinks: 'If only I had one  of those then I will be winning.' When in fact a fool who obtains a Bentley will still be a fool with a Bentley. These things are beautiful  and  demonstrate good taste, and even hard work, however they will  never be proof of manhood. They will never add true value to your existence or give meaning to life. Only the responsibility of leading a  family and guiding the destiny of other human beings and yourself can give you purpose. It is here you learn  that there are things worth  living  or dying for, and  cars, clothes, or jewelry will never amount  to that.

The drug dealer who makes five thousand dollars a day, but runs the streets and parties with multiple women is no match for the drug dealer who makes five hundred dollars a day and goes home at a set time to his family, where he rests, eats, and thinks about his next move. All criminals know this to be accurate. The person who never leaves the block or is always in the mix of things usually has the least money. He is also prone to mistakes and major blunders. On the other hand, the person who is barely seen makes hustling look easy.

Additionally, when he is caught, the dealer with a family is more likely to assess his errors and magnitude of his actions and correct them. He is likely to have a support network while incarcerated, and a network to help him when released. Furthermore he will know that whatever he has accumulated in assets will not be stolen or wasted. In the least he will know that his children are in good hands and not left with those who will take advantage of them. On the other hand the persistent nomad who cannot lay down roots and is committed to no family is likely to have no one committed to him. Thus every stage of his life is desperate, bitter, lonely and depending on someone else. I use this example to demonstrate that it does not matter how low your profession is this rule is universally applicable; family life provides everyone who enters it a distinct advantage.

Those with stable homes who take care of responsibilities are mentally, emotionally, and intellectually better positioned than those who think that freedom comes from the unchained pursuit of pleasure. This stability not only translates into wealth but has rewards that cannot be quantified. Those in stable relationships and those not, also produce different kinds of offspring. Nobody except the most delusional thinker will disagree that children raised in homes where they have access to two parent are (on average) better off. They are also less likely to struggle with poverty and be better positioned socio-economically. Thus, reducing their chances of entering the world as desperate male predators with intellects straining to interpret phenomenon, or as  approval seeking young women accustomed to partaking in debauchery for survival.

Those who cannot settle down with a solitary mate and form a deep bond  are prone to self-destruction, social conflict, disorganization,  or disease. Much of the misery that Blacks in the hood face is born in the wombs of poorly  educated single-teen mothers who have nothing to give a child except hate, pain, confusion, and frustration. The Black male must understand that power is not derived from "money, and respect" but the organization of his resources and  priorities. Power rests in the way a man manipulates his environment beginning with himself; it is  discipline and  sacrifice. Power is found in the balance  between ambition, hard work, responsibility, mastery, leisure, and rest. Power comes from networking with other stable, dependable, and family-orientated people. Dependable people are those whose homes you can visit, not people who are hard to find or unreliable and unpredictable.  A person who is not committed to family can have no sense of duty, obligation or maturity,  and without these things a male remains a boy.  Boys cannot be trusted with responsibilities to carry out orders or to know the meaning of brotherhood. Boys do not understand manhood. Boys break everything they touch, are unstable and irresponsible. Boys cannot run businesses,  neighborhoods, communities, or anything lesser or greater. The clear difference between a man and a boy is a man maintains a stable household and a boy runs the street and plays with toys and friends.

Without the sense of duty and obligation a male will never experience the invigorating  energy that follows  commitment and dedication to family.  They will lack the energy  and motivation to succeed that only comes from knowing others depend on you. A man who has never had others rely on him for their food, shelter, and safety has never led a life  with purpose. Young  Black males must be taught and  made to embrace family life as something more than morally right, but as  something that leads to power, wealth, and health. Family life is cool because  it is what people who have power use to perpetuate themselves.  Family life is the only way to power.

Likewise young women must be taught the meaning of family life and the techniques for maintaining a stable home. We must understand that the models that men and women use will at times be polygamous or monogamous depending of their religious and social needs; we need not be locked into the western ideal of family structure as we need a family scheme that will fulfill our cultural, economic, and emotional needs. The model best suited for raising healthy children and living a life of power.

We need to destroy these images of death that have come to dominate our self-conception. Images of pimps  and players cannot be praised anymore; pimps are filthy diseased ridden people who should be purged wherever they are  found, not celebrated as models of real men. Most pimps end their legacy as  they began - as  junkies. We have pre-pubescent  children mimicking the walk and talk of pimps and prostitutes; we should be ashamed of ourselves that we laugh at this as  'cute or funny.' We have normalized the worst manifestation of culture - we celebrate our own demise with amusement. Boys must be taught that a gang is  a destructive fraternal organization  built and maintained by exploitation, manipulation, and domination of the weak - it is not a family. Girls must be taught that a family is not  when a bunch of friends live together and raise a baby.

Black culture is not static or fixed but fluid we are not going back to retrieve all the African customs we can find in order to reassemble the Black man like Humpty Dumpty. We are new people, modern people not bound by history or stereotypes. That said, family is a constant, it is the building block of all other organizational power. It has been with  us at every evolutionary stage of human development. This is the most sacred  social unit of primordial people and continues to be  a durable  institution that  confers benefit to those who subscribe to it.

We must reorganize ourselves as a people in  order to survive and the first order of business is for us to organize ourselves into  family units to ensure that our health, wealth, and sanity is maintained. Family is not a luxury that we can do without or do away with, but a necessity if we are to be mentally stable, and socially productive  rulers of this planet. Those who disagree will find themselves and their progeny at the bottom of every measure of progress - whether in wealth, health, education, intelligence, power, goodness, or organizational ability. Seventy years of proof has shown they will produce the most destruction prone children; also the most mentally ill, physically ailing, powerless, easily manipulated, resentful, emotionally confused, and  pitiful human beings.

Those who disagree will  invite  into their homes the grim reaper. They will produce offspring who are burdens to their family, friends, society, and civilization itself. There is no other way to heal ourselves except through the formation of family. There is no governmental policy to attack, no racist to point at, no marching, crying or shopping  our way out of this misery. There is not enough government reparations  in the world that can replace  what has been taken. There is no way  to revenge our way back  to health. If the Democrats and  Republicans promise to make you equal they are lying; they  cannot make broken and disorganized people equal- nobody can - it is utterly impossible.

If we want to be free and strong all roads lead to family. If we want to beat the  system and overcome the overwhelming odds stacked against us, we have to organize ourselves into stable family units and breed excellence into the world. There is no party, gang, car, house, neighborhood,  gun, or ideology that can save us - there is only the family. And this will remain true until the world stops turning and the lord calls all souls back for judgment

Tehuti the Scribe

Completed December 2022

This book is dedicated to Sandra Farakahn 1946-2022

# NOTES


THE PURPOSE AND PRESENCE OF HISTORY

1.  Crawford v. Washington 541 U.S. 36 (2004)

2.  At The End of an Age by. John Lukas pg. 159.

3. Nietzsche Philosopher, psychologist, anti Christ by, Walter Kaufmann Fourth Edition, Princeton New Jersey Princeton University Press Copyright 1974 pg. 211.

4.  Nietzsche ibid at 145

5. Bob Marley SEPTEMBER 2015 EBONY Interview of Bob Marley  conducted in September 1980 by Nelson George pg. 116 EBONY September 2015

6.  Suketu Mehta TIME Magazine  February 3, 2014 pg. 35-39.

MANY SHADES of  VICTIMOLOGY &  METHODS OF COPING

7.  ONYX "2 wrongs" All WE GOT IS US,  1996.

8. Nietzsche Philosopher, psychologist, anti-Christ by, Walter Kaufmann Fourth Edition, Princeton New Jersey Princeton University Press Copyright 1974 pg. 143.  9. Ibid at 145

9. Ibid.

10. THE AFRICAN ORIGIN OF CIVILIZATION Myth or Reality, Cheikh Anta Diop Lawrence Hill Books Copyright © Presence Africaine, 1955 and 1967. First edition February, 1974 Lawrence.

11. Harriet Washington Medical Apartide "The Dark History of Medical Experimentation on Black Americans from Colonial Times

to the Present". Published by Anchor Books, A division of Random house, Inc., New York pg. 21, 22.

12. New York Times article December 19, 2021

13. Lonnie Bunch Smithsonian Magazine Smithsonian magazine issue entitled:  "Blacks in America"/  September 2016.

14. Abdul  Karim  Hasan,  Our Family's Evolution from Nationalism to Al-Islam, published by Bait-Cal 2019

15. Sherman A. Jackson, Islam and the Blackamerican, Looking toward the Third Resurrection Sherman A. Jackson, *Islam and the Blackamerican* `LOOKING TOWARD THE THIRD RESURRECTION, Oxford University  press copyright 2005 by University press, Inc. Sherman A. Jackson is  a Scholar in Islamic Studies etc. Islam and the Blackamerican is a book that purports to be for African Americans but on closer scrutiny the book is far too academic to be written as a guide for this class of persons. It falls into that line of literature that I suggest is not written for Blacks but about them. I found Sherman's analysis lacking in other areas, for example, he goes into lengths about the origins, history and direction of Islam in America among blacks, but he does not once mention the prison system. In any advent Jackson seems to support my theory that the Islam that is being taught to Black people is arresting their development when it comes to their ability to maneuver the social reality of America, and that any form of the religion that excludes our historical, ethnic, racial, political reality will never be accepted.

16. Alex Haley, The Autobiography of Malcolm X pg. 259-262

17. Abdul  Karim  Hasan,  Our Family's Evolution from Nationalism to Al-Islam, published by Bait-Cal 2019

18. Ibid

19. Mobb Deep An Eye for an Eye

19. ONYX all We got is us (1996)

20.  Interview with Lil Wayne by Lindsey Davis Nightline ABC November 1, 2016

21.  Nightline interview with Camron.

22. The Secret Teachings of All ages Manly P. Hall Copyright 2003 by Philosophical Research Center Penguin group USA inc 315 Hudson  street New York NY 10014 pg 249-255

23.  The Secret Teaching Ibid.

MOYNIHAN

The Broken Black Family

1. The Moynihan Report 1965.

 Condemnation of Blackness Race, Crime and the making of Modern Urban America by Khalil Gibran Muhammad Harvard University  Press Copyright 2010 Fellows of Harvard college pg, 172; citing James S. Stemmons 'Why crime Increases among Negroes", Philadelphia Ledger may 10, 1907 reprinted in Colored American magazine July 1907, pg 65-68.

2. Just-Ice "welfare recipient" The Desolate one 1987. Just -Ice is often cited as being the first ganster rapper.

3. Coates Article appeared in The Atlantic and was titled "the Black Family in the age of Mass incarceration" Http: www. theatlantic.com/magazine/archive/2015/10/the-black-family in-the - age- of- mass-incarceration/ 4032461.

4.  Ibid.  Gunnar Myrdal cited by Coates

5.  The Isis Papers Keys to the colors, by Frances Cress Welsing 1991 Third world  press, Chicago Pg. 267-68.

THE SOURCE OF ALL POWER

FAMILY IS THE FIRST LEVEL OF SELF ORGANIZATION IN A COMMUNITY

6.  A History of Rome to A.D. 565 Arthur E. R. Boak & William G. Sinnigen  pg. 89 copyright 1921, Seventh printing 1970  The MACMILLAN  Company.

7. AFRICANA The Encyclopedia of the African American Experience  copyright 1999 Editors Kwame Anthony Appiah Harvard University Henry Louis Gates Harvard University. Egyptian Mythology pg. 670.

8. The History of Japan By R.H.P. Mason and J.G. Caiger Charles E. Tuttle Company, Inc. of Rutland, Vermont and Tokyo Japan Copyright 1972 Sixteenth printing 1990. Pg.3.

9. Dreams Of Africa in Alabama The Slave ship Clotilda and The Story of the Last Africans bought to America. By Sylvia A  Diouf. OXFORD UNIVERSITY press 2007. Pgs. ????

10. SOCIOLOGY Explaining the Architecture of Everyday life By David M. Newman Fourth edition Copyright 2002 by sage Publication, Inc. Pg. 26..

11.  The Basic Writings of Nietzsche Translated and Edited by Walter Kaufmann Copyright 2000 pg.144, 145

12.  Ibid. Dreams Of Africa in Alabama The Slave ship Clotilda and The Story of the Last Africans bought to America. By Sylvia A Diouf.  OXFORD UNIVERSITY press 2007. Pgs. ? The text  I read from was not numbered

13.  THE WARMTH OF OTHER SUNS The Epic Story of America's Great Migration by Isabel Wilkerson First Vintage Books Edition Copyright 2010 pg. 265 citing Thomas C. Wilson "Explaining Black Southern Migrant Advantage in family stability: "the role of selective migration" social forces 80, no. 2 (December 2001) 555-71

14.  Ibid at pg. 261 citing E. Franklin Frazier " The Negro Family in Chicago" 1939 Chicago University of Chicago press 1932     pg. 80, 84..

15. AMERICAN LEGAL HISTORY (ALH) Second Ed Cases and Materials Kermit L. Hall, William M. Wiecek, Paul Finkelman Oxford University Press 1991, 1996 Copyright Oxford University Press Inc. Pg. 286

16. Ibid  pg. 286 citing  Charles Loring Brace "The Causes of Crime" 1880.

17.  Isis Papers Ibid at 272